50 Days in Europe

Two People – One Caravan – No Plan

Inpursuitofadream.com
our caravan adventures

Deb Ludford

For my Mum, Mavis because I can't get her to go online and our children, Emily & Alice for feeding Oscar the Cat

Copyright © 2017 Deb Ludford

All rights reserved.

ISBN: 9781976714016

50 Days in Europe

Deb Ludford

Contribution

Steven Ludford

Front Cover Artwork

Steven Ludford

Contents

Forward   ….. 6

Eurotunnel in a Caravan   ….. 7

Turn left towards Belgium & The Netherlands   ….. 10

Wulpen Camping, Cadzand, The Netherlands – Site Review   ….. 14

Keukenhof -The Garden of Tulips... and People   ….. 16

The 'Low' Lands and 'Highs' of Amsterdam   ….. 19

Koole Kampeerhoeve, Noorden, The Netherlands – Site Review ….. 22

Half Timber Houses & Sausages   ….. 24

Herkules Bergpark, Wilhelmshöhe, Kassel   ….. 28

Camping in Naumburg, Germany – Site Review   ….. 30

Washing day   ….. 32

The Cute and Brute of Germany   ….. 34

Camping Paradies Franken, Germany – Site Review   ….. 38

Old Romantics   ….. 40

Camping Erlebnis Zugspitze, Germany – Site Review   ….. 44

Austria in the Caravan   ….. 47

Natterer See, Innsbruck, Austria – Site Review   ….. 52

Lake Garda, so hard to leave   ….. 55

Camping Fossalta, Lake Garda, Italy – Site Review ….. 60

Two Tour Tuscany ….. 62

Piazza People Watching ….. 68

Barco Reale, Tuscany, Italy – Site Review ….. 70

Van to SanRemo & No-Go Monaco ….. 72

Camping Vallecrosia, Italy – Site Review ….. 76

Arrivederci Italy, Bonjour France, Howdy America ….. 78

La Sousta, Pont du Gard, France – Site Review ….. 81

Massif Central, Troglodytes and Templar Knights ….. 83

Le Papillon, La Cresse, France – Site Review ….. 87

Lazy Ladybird Days & Six Inches on a Map ….. 89

La Coccinelle, Blot l'Église, France – Site Review ….. 92

Last days of the trip ….. 94

Saint Nicolas Campsite, Brionne, France – Site Review ….. 98

50 for 50 - Our European Tour Summary ….. 100

You want to caravan abroad, but … ….. 102

Forward

For my 40th birthday we had a night at the Theatre, 'Les Misérables' and a flight on The London Eye. I wondered what was planned for my 50th birthday. In a moment of madness, Steve, aka 'The Boss' suggested we celebrate our joint arrival at 50 with 50 days touring Europe in our caravan, '50 for 50'.

One of the few perks of a zero hours contract enabled 'The Boss' to free the time and I received permission for a non-paid holiday of a lifetime. It was going to happen.

Caravan owners for only two years and generally the type to plan every detail of a holiday to ensure no stone unturned. Not this time, we decided to book the channel crossing from UK to France, the first night caravan site, the return channel crossing and no more. We were going to 'wing it' with the help of an 'off season' caravan site phone App and no more. Going clockwise on the map of Europe was our only concession to planning.

All these chapters originally appeared as articles published in our www.inpursuitofadream.com caravan blog. Photographs for each article can be found on the relevant blog pages, however, we have found the text only versions within this book have opened up a flavour of the trip that allows the imagination of the reader to take over.

Eurotunnel in a Caravan

This is our second caravan trip to Europe and on both occasions, we have gone via Eurotunnel. We have looked at ferry alternatives but on balance, the cost, frequency of trains, easy boarding, speed of crossing and ability to stay with car/caravan make it a no-brainer for us.

Once again, we paid for the trip, OK, 50% of it, with our Tesco Clubcard reward points. We achieve this purely through use of a Tesco credit card paid off "In Full" every month. The reward points used to be higher and the rewards better but Tesco have realised too many people, like us, don't darken their doors or pay interest on their credit. I digress, anyway £50 reward points is tripled to £150 towards our train tickets.

Leaving the M20 at J11a you follow the cars (not the Trucks) to the automated check-in booths, the touch screen process is simple because the camera recognises your car registration and just asks you to confirm your booking, including option to switch to earlier crossing, which we accepted. It prints a ticket 'hanger' with a large printed letter (we were 'P') that is your crossing identifier. You hang this from your rear-view mirror, ultimately it gets scanned by an attendant on the train.

Now rest, if you have time, the next part looks like a motorway service station but no reversing required. You park up while large boards indicate the status, in English and French, of each 'Letter' to proceed or await boarding. The timing is quite accurate so you may have time for a big 'Full English' or some last-minute travel accessories.

Your turn, the board display informs you to proceed for boarding, there is a big 'To France' direction sign to help guide you, not that you have any other option at this point. Next is Passport control and security. A small ten-minute queue today for us, not sure what kid's holidays would be like. Only two lanes open today, a French car to our left tried to jump lanes, the Brits bristled and suddenly glued their bumpers to each other. So funny really, everyone is ending up on the same train anyway plus I realised she was obviously Left-Hand Drive and our lane was being served left side.

A big hand of authority said 'Stop'. "Please drive into Lane 2 to be checked" while all the solo cars headed for the train. I had pictures in my mind of rubber gloves in a private room, no, "can you open your Gas locker so we can check the gas tanks are closed", phew, "have a good day".

Nearly there, one last point where they calculate the length of your outfit and tell you which lane to await final boarding. Then wait for green lights and head for the train.

Until you first board a train you will probably worry about boarding, don't, the access point is very generous giving plenty of room to get straight for the drive through each carriage. Keep a couple of car lengths back from the vehicle before you and hang back when they slow/stop as you may not fit in the same carriage as them, the staff will guide you. Then stop, handbrake on, engine off, select 1st gear, windows half way down, relax.

We got in the caravan and cracked open the butties and pies whilst enjoying the journey in comfort, admittedly, it was rocking a bit. No sooner had we finished the butties and sunlight of the French variety was flooding into the carriage.

Departing is easier than boarding, you drive out the front end of the train and without being stopped again are filtered directly to the French motorway routes. If it's your first time 'on the right' you will be anxious but signage is good and junction entries/exits extend better than UK ones so you have more time to merge, within minutes you will wonder why you worried.

We will probably make use of a surface sea crossing one day in the future, maybe for Spain, but for now Eurotunnel gets our vote.

Turn left towards Belgium & The Netherlands

Packed the caravan and sorted everything out in the days leading up to the trip. Quick shower. Wave goodbye to our grown-up jellybeans and the cat, in the car on the way to the storage site by 8am.

50 minutes after the start of our drive we were still only 18 miles down the road stuck in rush hour traffic on the A3 as the paper pushing masses try to get behind their desks in Guildford by 9am. The rest of the drive to the Channel Tunnel went smoothly. We arrived early and even managed to book onto an earlier train.

Quick toilet stop in the terminal before boarding, surprisingly very quiet today. Within 40 minutes of arriving we are safely cosseted in our own carriage for the 30 minutes or so journey. Butties for lunch eaten in the caravan. Freshly fed and watered, France starts to flicker into view through the carriage windows.

Right hand side of the road and the sun is out, so being the wind, it's blowing a hooley and The Boss grumbles about how the caravan is blowing around. Onto smaller roads and the weather calms and driving becomes easier. France becomes Belgium, the landscape stays the same but to our uneducated eyes the road signs are now in an unfamiliar language. Out of our comfort zone now. We can manage in France both verbally and with the written word. Now I feel lost trying to second guess what words might mean. Belgium gives way to Holland. No signage declaring a change of country, no obvious border, just our first windmill standing proud in the vastness of flat farmland.

The site is easy to find and we are welcomed in fluent English by the two lovely wardens. Pitched up, unpacked and kettle on within our usual half an hour. Wi-Fi on site so my worry of not being able to contact the jellybeans is gone. I've checked in, we've arrived safe and sound. Something out of the freezer at home for tea tonight, gammon and leek pie hungrily devoured. Now to get the bike out of the car.

The wind is still blowing and is quite cold around the head. Having piled the pounds on recently the usual lycra cycling gear has been left at home, we didn't want to frighten the locals. A scenic ride down to the coast, a sandy beach and small marina. Very blowy, with temperatures dropping rapidly as the evening draws in. Riding a bike in Belgium/The Netherlands is a joy, cycle lanes are separated from traffic almost everywhere and are not an afterthought like the UK, where they paint a white line on the pavement that stops at every side road or allocate the rain gutters of the road to cyclists. Cyclists and Car Drivers don't need to hate each other here, due to intelligent planning they barely meet.

Heavy rain overnight and the world is looking freshly watered. It was looking slightly parched and is now revitalised. On the agenda today, back into Belgium to visit Bruges. It's like taking a step back in time, architecturally. Ornate buildings of all shapes and sizes skirt round pretty squares. Now, though is not the time for sightseeing, The Boss is busting, he needs a wee and he needs one soon. As with everything you can never find a loo when you need one. We march across squares, up and down streets. Not a loo in sight. Normally we'd pop in a Costa or McDonald's. It seems the part of Bruges we are now frantically pacing is too posh for these kinds of establishments. Whilst walking we're also on the lookout for lunch, it's now past lunchtime and he's hungry too. Posh nosh is on offer, with prices to make The Boss push his wallet further into his pocket. Toilet located in an underground car park. 0.40€ each for a wee. Money flung at the nice lady and in we run.

Now to find food, with nothing obviously on offer we spy a small shop and grab a chicken wrap each. Wander around the next corner to be presented with an array of street food stalls, just the kind of thing we fancied, typical. Just so that we didn't feel too fed up we treated ourselves to a heavily loaded sugar infused waffle.

Back to the car, on a complete sugar high, supermarket needed for supplies. This is where the day gets worse. A Carrefour looms on the right with 2 spaces outside. In we go, not one of the cheapest of supermarkets we have come across so we only pick up the absolute essentials. Lidl, where are you when we need you?

As we pull away I notice a piece of paper flapping beneath the wiper blade. "Probably some discount voucher" says The Boss, I'm not so sure, we pull over so I can retrieve it. The sheer amount of red ink immediately suggests this is not a discount voucher, it's a parking ticket. Unlike the UK, where a parking restriction is clearly marked by road lines and lamp-post signs, we had driven into a permit parking zone signposted about half a mile previous, we should have seen it, yes, but in a strange environment your driving senses are foremost on safety and positioning rather than parking permits. 30€ to be paid in 30 days, Thanks Bruges it's been nice knowing you. Guess what, lovely little Lidl around the corner complete with car park.

Back at the site and they are celebrating the King's birthday, a public holiday. The campsite has issued a free alcoholic drink voucher for all guests, seems a shame to waste it so off we trot armed with our voucher clutched in sweaty palm. We are hot on the heels of our Dutch neighbours who very graciously give up any chance of a good afternoon chatting to friends to keep the English couple next door from being 'Billy No Mates'. We 'clicked' instantly with Max & Carla (we think that was their names) who seemed to have a similar outlook and sense of humour about life. A few more drinks followed until the temperature dropped and The Boss realised his stomach was nudging him in the ribs for a top up (ie. his Tea).

Our new Cadac made its debut tonight, Butterfly Chicken, Sausage and Vegetables flung in the Paella Pan and left to sizzle. The Boss pretended he was cooking by turning everything over every half minute, I left him to it. It was bloody good though, I let him think it was due to his cooking prowess.

After two nights it's time to move on, we have a date with ex-Neighbours who live in Amsterdam coming up. Max & Carla had created a list of highly recommended sites in France for later on our tour, plus advice for today's planned route and we chatted a little more. Lovely people, if everyone else we meet is only half as nice, it will be a good trip.

Wulpen Camping, Cadzand, The Netherlands – Site Review

Situated in Cadzand, this is a lovely well laid out site. Wulpen Camping, just over the border after Belgium into the Netherlands makes this an ideal stopping point on your way to or from the UK and only two hours from Calais.

The wardens greeted us in fluent English and directed us to our pitch. Typically, you see caravans pitched sideways in Mainland Europe with awnings facing forward. We were about to motor-move the caravan into position when the site manager passed with electric buggy and offered to pitch our caravan for us. OK, why not?

The site has individually hedged, fully serviced, grass pitches and well planted grounds. Car parking is situated close to pitches. With a good mix of statics, seasonal and touring pitches, the site is well planted and set out. Wulpen caters for all ages, with a lovely park for children and games facilities including table tennis, bar football, boules and a volleyball pitch there is even a small bar and onsite shop selling basic groceries.

The site also offers cycle hire. Situated close to the beach and with a perfect cycling infrastructure there's no reason not to cycle even if you don't have your own bike. Perfectly flat too, so easy riding.

There is a heated toilet and shower block (free hot showers) with laundry and dishwashing facilities. Wifi is free and works well across the site. We used the ACSI off season discount with our booking and for a small discount. Would we come again? Yes! Although we only stayed for 2 nights we could gladly have stayed longer.

Keukenhof - The Garden of Tulips... and People

Beautiful sunny day predicted by the weather app, rain tomorrow. With only 2 days before we pack up the caravan and head towards our next destination we decide that today is the day to visit the 'tulips of (just south of) Amsterdam'.

It seems that the world, his wife and his dog looked at the forecast and thought the same thing. We should have realised that it was going to be busy as we sat for an hour in traffic on our way there. Once at the gardens, we were guided into a field of different coloured, shiny... cars. The biggest car park we've ever had the pleasure of parking in. Look for a landmark so that we can locate our car on our return. Motorhomes are welcome and rows of them stood to attention looking like the forecourt of a prestigious dealer.

Keukenhof is described in the expensive and not really needed guide book as 'The most beautiful spring garden in the world.' Boasting millions of flowering bulbs, it really is spectacular. The park opened its gates in 1950 and to this day is a popular attraction. The garden has multiple indoor halls displaying plants and flowers in addition to the acres of outdoor beds. To add to the blasts of colour as far as the eyes can see, sculptures, fountains and babbling brooks are dotted around. In a small part of the gardens there is also a small petting area where you are encouraged to walk with the turkeys and watch the pot-bellied pigs snuffling around in the mud. Boat trips glide past fields of flowering bulbs. A windmill stands proud in the gardens, people queue to enter and climb to its viewing platform.

The gardens are wheelchair and pram friendly and dogs are welcomed within the grounds. There are food stalls selling everything you could possibly want from strawberries and burgers to the humble bottle of water. Toilets are located at the entrance before you pay. Smaller queues for the ladies where found inside the halls in the gardens themselves.

Beautiful brides posed amongst the floral delights, whilst family members stood and oohed and ahhed. I wonder if they all paid to get in? Expensive photo shoot if they did.

This is where I digress, whilst the gardens are stunningly beautiful they are spoiled by people. Flower to flower people. Bumped and shoved as people with cameras bigger than any used by the BBC try to aim and shoot to get the perfect shot of stamen within purple petals. Imagine, a Rolling Stones stadium concert at kicking out time. Shoulder to shoulder, bustling for the exit. This goes on and on throughout the gardens. Shuffling, pausing en mass to admire a bed of tulips in all their splendour. Peaking between heads of the people in front of you to see why we've stopped this time. Stopping suddenly as someone way ahead pauses without warning to take a selfie. Too many people in my personal space for me to fully appreciate nature's splendid beauty.

With a €6 parking charge, €16 per person to get in and €5 for the guide book, this has started to get expensive because after only two hours we can't cope and are heading for the exit. The place is stunning and with only two months of visual delights is always going to be busy, our advice, try to go on a weekday out of any holiday period. Even then it will attract the masses, there just maybe, if you're lucky, a few less.

Keukenhof is only open to the public for eight weeks of the year. This year it's final day is 3rd May, 2017. Next year the opening dates are 22nd March to 21st May, 2018. For us, this goes on the same list as New York, love that we got to see it, but would not bother a second time. Take that as a weird recommendation.

The 'Low' Lands and 'Highs' of Amsterdam

The wind was blowing a hooley as we headed north on the second leg of our trip, our Dutch neighbour 'Max' said it would not be too windy to take the coastal route, I think the Dutch must be more hardened to the wind judging by the colour of The Boss' knuckles holding onto the steering wheel. After passing through the 4-mile-long Western Scheldt Tunnel (€7.45 for car/caravan) we stopped for our dinner by the water's edge at Neeltje Jans.

The motorways of Rotterdam gave The Boss brain ache whilst battling the traffic, the wind and foreign language directions. Not that he moans, or I couldn't hear him as I dozed. Off the motorway and almost instantly onto single track roads through sleepy villages. Not too sleepy though, oncoming traffic slowed our journey down to almost a crawling standstill. Sat Nav turns us left and right and then straight ahead, I'm sure she's lost.

Koole Kampeerhoeve is a sharp left turn in what appears to be a small town of quite pretty houses. First impressions of the site, not as impressed initially as I was at the last site. This site is more of a CL but houses more than 5 'vans. Very open aspect with the biggest skies you can imagine. The view through the rectangle window is vast giving way to beautiful sunsets and for those who know me, I got the biggest sky imaginable, I love a big sky.

Off to the local supermarket for a few bits, the cashier took one look at our plastic and rapidly shook his head as though it were explosive. Coppering up for a bottle of wine, is just what we hadn't planned on doing.

After a good night's sleep, we went in search of a cash machine and a Lidl in the next town, Woerden. Had a laugh later when one of our Jellybeans was surprised they had a Lidl in Europe. A lovely, traffic free ride on the tandem took us 10 miles to Uithoorn, a purpose to this trip, visiting old friends and neighbours, who moved back here 2 years ago. Fantastic catch up, great chat and lovely food provided by Marcel, Sam and their now grown up daughter, Melissa. A plan was hatched to ride into Amsterdam the next day, Marcel generously offered to drive us back to caravan, nice chap, so we could leave tandem with them overnight to make the ride shorter from their house.

Now Sunday, with forecast for rain on Monday, The Boss decided we had a busy day. Keukenhof Tulip Gardens was a 'must see' attraction and we would drive there before doing the tandem ride to Amsterdam later. Ambitious plan. One hour sat on the approach to Keukenhof while a road bridge lifted up and down every time a boat came near didn't help much. Keukenhof was beautiful in the sunshine but was unbelievably busy, after only two hours our crowd claustrophobia had us heading for the car park.

Car swapped for Tandem and we are again riding along dedicated cycle lanes into the heart of Amsterdam, the contrast to riding in UK is immense, big tick to Dutch planning. Amsterdam centre is unsurprisingly busy, we have ridden in London and Paris also, so find the navigation and slow pace bike balance OK. If you rode in with children it would perhaps be wise to lock up the bikes and walk the manic central areas. We stop for a beer, The Boss picks an empty bar, why? The coffee shop next door looks far more popular. We are served quickly so I don't complain. 'Smokeys' next door is definitely 'smokin' and we are soon passively enjoying the atmosphere and feeling just a little more 'happy' than expected. Oh yes, we are in Amsterdam, silly us.

A lazy day followed the busy day. After 25 miles in the saddle yesterday my derrière is a little tender, we really should use the bike more often, those Brooks saddles are so hard on the unaccustomed backside. Butties, northerners remember, made on bakery fresh nutty bread. I hate homemade butties but these were delicious. Relaxing reading a book, we even sat out in the late afternoon with Dutch appetisers and a glass of Amstel, thanks Sam.

As we planned tomorrow's drive to Germany a Heron flew past bringing the day to a close.

Koole Kampeerhoeve, Noorden, The Netherlands – Site Review

Koole Kampeerhoeve is situated in a small town with a supermarket, bakery and other shops within a 10-minute walk away. This site is central to Amsterdam, Utrecht, Rotterdam, The Hague and the beautiful gardens of Keukenhof Tulip Gardens.

The site is made up of about five small fields linked together, each with about half a dozen flat grass pitches. If you can get on the furthest field you are treated to the most amazing views, sunsets and sky-scapes. The view from our pitch had to have the biggest sky I've ever seen. Caravans, Motorhomes and tents are welcome. Each pitch has its own 6amp EHU point and the fresh water tap is a short walk away.

A small clean and heated toilet block is located near the car park. Showers are clean and heated but are chargeable, being a bit tight, we chose to use our own shower in the caravan. Outdoor dishwashing facilities and a chemical disposal are also available. No grey waste apparent on site, locals seem to be watering the bushes. As with a few European sites we have come across pitches are car free so after unloading you are required to park in the designated areas.

A small play area is located at the edge of the site for children and the caravan park entrance leads immediately onto traffic free cycle lanes leading to local towns and villages.

This site is also part of the ACSI discount scheme.

Half Timber Houses & Sausages

Our need for a washing machine and Wifi dictated our next stop of the tour. So, we find ourselves deep into Germany near the City of Kassel.

Camping in Naumberg is to be our home for the next few days. Again, more than happy with first impressions of the site, this might have had something to do with the dog that insisted on having its tummy tickled and it's ears rubbed as we check in.

I have only one or two words in my German repertoire and The Boss, although he studied German at school now informs me that he didn't listen and only knows a few words more than I do. Time to muddle on. I'm sure even we can order two beers!

An hour spent on Google, The Boss has found us something to do, best be sharp we haven't got long. He's pulling jumpers out of the wardrobe, grabbing coats and cameras. Come on hurry, get in the car, you're going to like this. Off we go. I hate not knowing what it is we are doing; did we need walking boots? Should we have picked up a bottle of water? Tutting he tells me to trust him and off we go. What cash have we got he asks, change for parking? Nope, I'd fed it all to the washing machine the previous evening. Tutting and shaking his head he sets off in another direction on the lookout for a shop. Water bought, €0.11 a bottle! We pay nearly a pound at home

Back in the car and we pull into a car park at the foot of a huge monument. A nice young man with a plug in his ear as big as the plug hole in my sink tries with success to converse in English.

€7 to park the car, see the attraction and some sort of bus ride for the two of us - bargain! The Boss loves a bargain, it'd best be good. Herkules BergPark, was I must admit spectacular and well worth the visit. The moaning that left my mouth when he suggested we walk back up the hill to the car rather than find the promised shuttle bus back up the biggest hill I've ever had the pleasure of walking down, isn't printable, I'm sorry.

A trip to the supermarket, Lidl, very different but very familiar. With a fridge full of different types of sausage, I decide we need to try them all. Having recently become the proud owners of a Cadac, I'm loving the food that we've been eating off it whilst on this trip and decide that German Sausages are going to be on our menu, by the looks of the trolley, for the next few weeks.

A walk into the town, the following dull and grey day. Almost ghost town like, but stunningly beautiful. Our day was instantly awash with colour. Large timber framed houses painted in all their glory. Not a café or a bar open in the entire town. It's not often The Boss is willing to part with a few coppers for a 'cup of tea and a slice of cake', a bit of Worzel Gummidge there for those of us old enough to remember. On this occasion his Euros stayed firmly in his wallet.

Next stop Fatima's Grotte, all the way up another hill. Built by pilgrims as recently as 1956 a local landmark that hosts religious services in May and October. The Boss said if his church had been like this he may have gone more.

After our evening meal, yes, sausages featured again, my personal holiday guide had found another local point of interest only ten miles down the road just beyond an upside-down house.

The Edersee Dam was built in 1914 submerging three villages in the process. Descendants of the villagers return to pay respects only when a long dry, hot summer reveals the sleeping buildings to the world. To many, the 'Eder Dam' is remembered for being breached by the 'bouncing bomb' in May 1943 and was fully rebuilt within months by thousands of workers diverted from construction of the 'Atlantic Wall'.

We take time to admire the imposing structure then are distracted by a fantastic 'hands on' educational water feature of Dams, Waterwheels and Waterfalls all fed by two Archimedes Screws which two big English kids, us, we're frantically turning.

For our final day in Naumburg we decide it's a Tandem day. The Boss had seen a potential route and ventured to ask reception if it was recommended, using his four German words, much arm waving and English words spoken with a German accent, as if it would help. Yes, it was recommended, but the friendly lady pointed out on the map the road from our site to the cycle trail saying "Das ist Shit", we understood that, so threw tandem in the Volvo and parked as recommended by a wonderful Pancake House.

The Ederseebhan cycle trail was good, at home these are often tunnels of dense trees. Today we are on a perfect Tarmac surface in beautiful open countryside, heading twelve miles to Korbach on a gradual 2% incline, he tells me the twelve-mile return will be freewheelin'. The only danger today is the risk of derailment by enormous snails.

We stop to eat our butties at a well-designed picnic area, in the near distance a road takes traffic at a brisker pace. As we look across, screech, skid, BANG, as a car slams into the side of another, then screech, skid, BANG, as the next car slams into the back of both. Quite a shunt, if the road had been quiet we may have had to run across and be, well, useless. Luckily for the unlucky there were more cars in attendance and help was at hand. Korbach was nice, but quiet, after a couple of laps round town we headed back before any rain could catch us. 2% decline back home freewheelin', wrong, the wind had different ideas and the ride back downhill was harder than the uphill ride. Back at Das Pfannkuchenhaus we surrendered and tucked into the biggest most delicious pancakes ever.

Heading South next......

Herkules Bergpark, Wilhelmshöhe, Kassel

Sat in the caravan, no plans today until The Boss looked up from his iPad and asked "What day is it?" We genuinely have lost track, and, "What time is it?" upon establishing it was Wednesday lunchtime he replied "Quick, let's get some food down us now, we need to be somewhere by 2.30pm."

It turns out that Kassel, only 30 minutes from our Naumburg caravan park, has an outstanding Hill-Park (Bergpark) of epic proportions. We parked at the top car park nearest to the Herkules statue at the very top of the hill. €7 paid for parking and access to the shuttle-bus back up the hill for two people. It was money well spent on both counts. Access to the park is totally free.

Still not knowing what to expect we rounded the Octagon/Herkules Monument to be both mesmerised and gutted at the same time. The view of the park and the City of Kassel beyond is staggering from this lofty position 350 metres above the Wilhelmshöhe Palace in the park below. Gutted? It seems the first part of the incredible show to follow is still under considerable maintenance and is postponed until mid-June 2017.

From May to early October, every Wednesday, Sunday and Public Holiday at 2.30pm 750,000 Litres of water are released from the Octagon/Herkules Monument to cascade down a long series of ornate platforms before continuing down through eight miles of watercourse that includes a further four spectacular water features, which today are open for us to enjoy. You walk from feature to feature just in time as the water reaches each one at a specified time culminating in a 50 metre Geyser/Fountain at the bottom.

Steinhöfer Waterfall: 3.05pm

Devil's Bridge: 3.20pm

Aquaduct: 3.30pm

Grand Fountain: 3.45pm

The whole park was designated a World Heritage Site in 2013. From the late 17th Century it was the summer residence of The Landgraves and later The Kings of Prussia and German Emperors. In effect, the whole park is a grand 'Folly' and a spectacular, beautiful one at that.

Be aware that this park involves a 350-metre walking descent so you do need to be good on your feet, didn't seem an issue for the hundreds of 60/70+ year old people around us today. Once we reached the bottom we followed the masses further downhill hoping they would lead us to a bus stop, that we hoped would be free, we really need to improve our German. We were in luck, a big 'H' bus stop loomed into view and some attempted German conversation with a local confirmed we would not be walking all the way back. The Boss sighed in relief, as did his ears.

Camping in Naumburg, Germany – Site Review

On the edge of a pretty little town the campsite is opposite a small water park, that in early May was still closed.

Arriving slightly out of hours, just after 5pm, the wardens buzzed us in and went through the booking in process with us. Once again, this site is part of the ACSI discount scheme. €15 deposit paid for the key fob for night time entry and exit to the site, this fob also opens the facilities block after dark and is the means of obtaining hot water in the showers, which are chargeable.

The toilet cubicles have to be the biggest I have ever seen; very clean and toilet paper of a decent quality is provided.
With a bathroom designed for people with disabilities and a baby room there are spacious laundry and washing up rooms. The washing machines and driers charge €0.50 per 15 minutes, reception have a stash of change for you to swap and by the look of a cupboard in the corner it appears that washing powder and fabric softener were supplied free of charge. The washing up room also came fitted with hot plates for cooking on.

Off we went, no allocated pitches, just choose one and set up. No need to inform them either which one you chose. Quite early into the site the layout is open and laid out in terraced cul-de-sacs. We choose one and have it all to ourselves. Fresh water taps seem to be placed, one tap for every six or so pitches. The odd cul-de-sac has one tap per pitch.

There is plenty of space to walk your dog and a small play area for the children complete with boat, car and tight rope.

A small snack bar and bar are located near the site entrance. As the season is only just starting the bar and snack bar are only open for a few hours on specified evenings.

The site itself is quite large with the foremost pitches for tourers and the furthest part of the site dedicated to seasonal caravanning. And by seasonal they really know how to do it in style with some wonderful structures and decking built around their 'vans.

The site also has the best chemical disposal we have ever come across. It was indoors and complete with hand washing sink, soap and paper towels.

At €72 for 4 nights using the ACSI discount card this is a site we'd recommend and return to.

Washing day

Two weeks into our trip and we're fast running out of warm clothes to wear. The weather hasn't been unkind to us but it hasn't been drying weather. At our last site I fed a pocket full of Euros into the washer and the drier in the hope of trying to keep us going for a few extra days in jeans and jumpers.

With 'The Boss' not liking taking his wallet out of the mothballs and spending money on the drier again, the first hint of sunshine and I was racing to beat the rest of the site to the solitary washing machine. As I entered the laundry I was pleased to see the machine standing quietly in the corner. At a charge of just €3 and a huge drum I took this as a bargain and decided to wash the lot if we weren't wearing it. Towels, jumpers, bedding, the lot went in. It does sound an ambitious sized drum doesn't it? I splashed out and did 2 loads.

We were quite lean on packing for this trip, 50 days is a long time and with not being able to predict the weather we packed for all eventualities but not much of anything. 2 jeans, 2 jumpers, 2 shorts and loads of vest tops, it's my age I'm hot even when it's cold. With the weather being rather inclement this meant we had more or less exhausted the winter wardrobe of all its contents.

First hint of warm weather and the jeans are in the washer and the shorts are being worn. Summer wardrobe for today, forecast shows that the jeans will be back on tomorrow.

So much washing means plenty of drying space is needed. Telescopic airer is pegged into the ground. The window airier is in place. I love seeing washing blowing in the wind. I remember my mum saying the best sight was a line full of clean white nappies.

So, the washing is blowing in the gentle breeze as the sun beats down. Until it's dry all jobs are done. Go on then, pour me a little glass of something whilst I wait.

The Cute and Brute of Germany

The Sun is shining bright, must be moving on day, just typical. Approx five hours easy Autobahn driving down to Bavaria. Beautiful open scenery that would be constantly up and down if it wasn't for the multitude of bridges smoothing our way across the valleys. We have been travelling with a bit of 'blue' in the toilet cassette between sites to avoid the fees for loos at service stations, because we are tight, yes, but also, we never have the right loose change when we are busting 'to go'. One good thing about the Autobahns in Germany is the parking/picnic areas that appear every mile or so, far better to relax for a brief moment in a semi-quiet picnic area using your own facilities.

We have ventured into new territory today, one that many tourers will already be comfortable with, but not us. We have set off south in a foreign country and have no idea where we are heading. 'Oh Crikey'. We tried to contact a couple of camping sites yesterday but no reply came back, so we are going to attempt the 'just turn up' method. The Boss reckons there are about four sites in our intended area and we will simply hit them in geographical order. We needn't have worried, the very first site, despite some local road closures/diversions greeted us as if this method was perfectly normal. Remember we are off season so advanced bookings are probably still a requirement in summer weeks. First impressions of Camping Paradies Franken are good, we are walked to our pitch by a lovely Lady who spoke perfect English and advised best pitch position for sunrise/sunset whilst still giving us free choice of van position, which seems to be the way at numerous European sites. The evening is warm so, after a quick drive to the supermarket for a boot full of wine and beer for about 50p, the Cadac is fired up for action and food and wine are consumed as we watched the sun go down.

Day two is a lazy day, a day of rest, it is Sunday after all. The weather isn't even good, in fact it's bloody awful, but The Boss has a couple of trips up his sleeve and we reckon are best for the next two forecasted 'cloudy' days. So, we rest, short paragraph.

Rothenburg ob der Tauber is picture postcard stunning and a popular tourist attraction on the Romantische Straße (Romantic Road). After five minutes using Google-Translate for all the words on the car park ticket machine we drop in the five-euro coins to obtain a 'day ticket'. In general, we are finding car parks and attractions in Germany good or reasonable value, unlike home where the phrases 'daylight robbery' and 'rip off' are often heard as prices are discovered. We are parked only feet from the medieval City Wall which we are walking along within the minute beneath a pitched narrow roof.

We are definitely in tourist territory now, German is no longer the only language heard and we speak English, of sorts, with some Americans, and properly with an English couple and their daughter touring in a bright pink VW camper van, they were about to start their second year, minimalist or what?

Everything about this medieval town is beautiful, the buildings, the signs, the cobbled streets. Cars are free to drive areas that look too nice for modern life, but after visiting a number of ghost like towns on this trip it added to the hustle and bustle.

Once again, being out of season came to our aid as we were able to freely walk around the souvenir/'tat' shops without trouble and take photographs without hundreds of tourists giving 'V' signs in our way. As we left, we passed a memorial for hundreds of Jews burned alive as they took shelter in the town Castle in the 13th Century, a historical pointer for the following days trip. Historical note, King Edward 1 ordered the removal of all Jews from England in 1290 that lasted over 300 years and England was the first country that required Jews to wear a badge, it colours our history too.

The Boss picked out Nuremburg for our next trip. As we travel around we like to see first-hand images we recall in our childhood. As an eight-year-old, World War Two was thirty years over, but in his mind Adolf Hitler and John Wayne were still fighting it out, mainly due to the limited TV schedules of the 70's. Stupidly, with hindsight, he once stayed awake in fear of his life when a relative and her German boyfriend baby-sat one evening.

Nuremburg's enormous Nazi Party Rallies (National Party Conventions) of the 1930's featured heavily in those childhood images and we discovered that the grounds still exist today. We parked up for free at the entrance to the Dokumentationzentrum (museum), parking the car remains the only stressful part of European touring for us, and paid €5 each for an audio phone self-guided tour through a section of the imposing unfinished Reichsparteitagsgelände Kongresshalle that houses exhibit and film archives predominantly following the political and social rise of the Nazi Party/Third Reich.

Without getting politically boring, whilst retrospectively the whole period and movement seems absurd, this place helps you realise how it arose from a perfect storm of various conditions post World War One and the hardships imposed on the German public. Perhaps the most poignant exhibit was the final video of real life experiences where civilians described the subconscious process of being drawn into and supporting a social movement whilst the subtle introduction of the War Machine was growing unnoticed amongst them.

The annual Nuremburg Party Rallies ended when the War started (1939's 'Rally of Peace' was cancelled at short notice), prior to this they were an annual propaganda 'battery charge' to the movement attracting over 700,000 to orchestrated events over the period of a week. We were joined today by a number of German school trips and we were genuinely amused that children of all nationalities find forced museum trips boring, no doubt they thought it was that funny bloke with the moustache from 100 years ago, a long way from The Boss hiding under his bed in 1975.

We left the museum and took the short walk to the Zeppelin Fields, a rather weird experience to stand in the footsteps of history looking at the vast arena, now looking ramshackled around the edges and converted into various sport fields, including a motor racing circuit, in the centre.

It is both understandable and a shame that the site is falling into disrepair, we get talking to a friendly American couple from Wisconsin and decide in America it would be a Shopping Mall and in the UK, it would be a money maker. We intuitively understood why it is as it is today and shared wartime stories passed down by our Fathers/Grandfathers when we were bored school kids as we walk away.

Last full day and the sun is out and warm, hooray, get the dirty washing in the washing machine, the order of the day is drink beer and sit in the sun. The site reviews all mention amazing homemade cakes so we wander to the onsite bar and enjoy a Strawberry/Chocolate Gateaux before returning to Sun and Beer at the caravan.

The contents of the fridge are flung in the Cadac for tea, just to lighten the caravan you understand. We were dubious about bringing the Cadac on tour but so far it has cooked every meal, tomorrow it will be cooking on the border with Austria.

Camping Paradies Franken, Germany – Site Review

A member of the ACSI discount scheme. We tried calling in advance but couldn't get the call to connect so took a chance and just turned up.

Welcomed by a gentleman who gestured for us to wait a moment. Off he scuttled and returned with a fluent English speaking young lady. Booked in and walked to the far end of the site which was to be home for the next few days. She informed us that hot water in the showers and Wi-Fi were free.

On site is a small terraced café/bar/restaurant with outdoor seating. It has been said that they do the most delicious, homemade cakes. The cakes were sampled on our final afternoon, a table on the terrace with a delicious homemade strawberry and chocolate cake, washed down in the sunshine with an ice-cold beer. Perfect.

The facilities are down an outside staircase underneath the café. There are separate rooms housing the toilets and showers. They are very clean and warm. There is also a dishwashing/laundry room with a €3 charge for use of the washing machine.

There is an accessible wet room for people with mobility problems next to reception. Reception sells an assortment of caravan related products including blue and pink loo and most importantly, beer. A baker, also delivers fresh bread daily to order every morning.

The site is set in a very peaceful setting and along with a bug hotel that was inhabited. Other nick-nacky bits adorn the site making it quite quirky. Hares can be spotted bounding around in the grass and wild flowers, one even walked past us as we sat out, who needs breakfast TV?

Pitches are level with EHU and fresh water taps located across the site. Recycling is taken to another level on this site with a coral of bins all clearly marked for recycling. Everything has a bin it can be put in.

A play area for children is near the main building. Complete with swings, climbing frame and slide and other bits and pieces.

The site is family run and also offer spa and massage treatments by appointment. With a price list outside their treatment room in the facilities block. Our ACSI covered 4kWh of electric per day after which we paid €0.60 per kWh, this was €3 per day extra for us but we needed our heater on in the evenings as temperature was unseasonably low. We paid €118 including electric and tourist tax for 5 nights. We would recommend this site and found ourselves staying an extra day.

Old Romantics

The Romantic Road (Romantische Straße) runs approximately 200 miles from Würzburg to Füssen linking 28 scenic historical towns along the way. Moving south towards the Alps we decided a leisurely romantic drive would be preferable to Autobahn tedium and the accompanying wobbles as vans pass our caravan at unrestricted speeds. While the scenery in parts is breath-taking, especially further south as the Alps loom into view, the majority of the three-hour journey was spent following convoys of HGVs travelling at exactly 40mph, quite dull and distinctly unromantic really.

The appearance of the mountains also heralded an increase in temperature forcing us to deploy our, currently temperamental, air-conditioning for the final run into Garmisch and our next tour site of Camping Erlebnis Zugspitze. Once again, the site was completely different to the preceding ones and seemed to be one third Motorhome Aire, one third Caravan/Motorhome Pitches, one third seasonal. The weather forecast for the next three days was atrocious but it was the same across the whole area so we planned to sit it out at this site and give up any chance of sightseeing. On that basis this stopover turned into a pleasant bonus.

A mandatory local tourist tax, Grrrr, got The Boss grumbling, included free bus and train tickets for the town, Hooray, and by gosh we intended to get our money's worth. To be truthful this turned out to our advantage, first, a bus ride from the campsite door into Garmisch for a quick mooch, admiring the buildings adorned with full facade murals and elaborate window frame murals.

Next, we headed for the town railway station to the furthest platform where a small three carriage Alpine train awaited to take us back past the campsite to Eibsee Lake at the foot of Germany's largest mountain, Zugspitze. For approx €50 each we could have continued up the mountain on the Zugspitzebahn Cog-Wheel train, had the skies been bright blue we would have considered paying this sum, we once baulked at a similar price to go up Mont Blanc before coughing up and enjoying one of the most amazing experiences of our lives. Not today, clouds were brushing the summit, and that weather forecast! Money stayed safely moth balled in his wallet.

A couple of photos at Lake Eibsee and this time back on the bus to the campsite door. No, The Boss has other ideas, he has spied an opportunity to row on the lake. I am not so sure, I see disaster, upturned boats, a cold swim and lost worldly goods. Too late, he is heading for the counter and in his best 'useless' German saying "Ruderboot, sechzig minuten bitte", to which the assistant responds, "No problem, nine euros please" in a Californian accent, clearly, we look English, must be the socks, sandals and knotted hanky. I even get told that I speak Oxford English, my Boltonian twang mustn't be very strong today.

As 'The Boss' rows us to the centre of the lake, in glorious sunny weather, he tells me how he has always wanted the romantic experience of rowing on a beautiful lake in silence but for the gentle sound of oars as they leave the water, and my heartbeat as I await the capsize. It was indeed beautiful, and even a little romantic to drift along in the shadow of Mount Zugspitze. Rowing back was less romantic and more Steve Redgrave as the wind was blowing against us and our time on the water was running down, even Californians need to clock-off work. Water was no longer gently dripping from oars and was now splashing everywhere as The Boss unsuccessfully pretended he wasn't sweating. Back just in time, California man dragged the boat out of the water and was next seen sat in front of us on the bus home.

Mr Itinerary Man, another nickname The Boss has picked up over the years had another plan the following day, which involved driving from Germany to Germany via Austria which also required a drive to the local petrol station for the Austrian 'road toll' Vignette we needed anyway for the next campsite, but first we take another free bus ride to nearby Grainau for a walk around the village before noon and our dinner.

After food we jumped in the car. He often tries to keep me in the dark, which is another way of saying there are steep hills to walk/ride and I would refuse to go. By god if I'd've known the hill I was going to climb I would've been moaning at breakfast rather than half way up it. Having a sat nav that was built before most of the roads in Europe adds to the mystery tour but within the hour we park up on the edge of Füssen to see an interesting stepped waterfall and gorge carved through the rocks two hundred years ago to save Füssen from floods.

A further five-minute drive and we spot the Fairytale Castle of Neuschwanstein Castle high on the hillside, I start to suspect the next part. Luckily, there are four large car parks and a visitor centre/ticket office nearer to the castle, actually there are two castles, Hohenschwangau Castle is in the same area and both are separated by a forty-minute walk, did I say walk? Climb up a Tarmac road.

We could have gone by horse drawn carriage but The Boss' mind and wallet have a 'no pain no gain' operating system. The car park was €6 for a day ticket and day tickets to both castles would have cost us approx €25 each, we had no intention to go in, partly because a long tour forces us to be selective with expensive attractions, but mostly because we find 80% of the experience and beauty is in the scenery and setting and the other 20% inside often looks like opulence and riches seen elsewhere but at a cost. To be clear, if we were longer in the area we would go in but we were quite happy today to look from outside.

As we walked (climbed) the hill I was convinced this was the Chitty Chitty Bang Bang Castle, later confirmed by Google and some Facebook friends, it also turns out to be an influence on the Cinderella Castle, 'bippity boppity boo'. Large horses pulled carriages up the hill leaving deposits as they went, no sooner had it landed when a drive-on road cleaner was sucking it away, I'd like to see that job description, 'Equine emissions clearance officer' maybe? We finally reached the castle only The Boss sees another path going further up the hill, he senses my limit is reached and without wishing to lose any more Romantic effect goes alone while I rest. He returns fifteen minutes later talking of breath-taking views for one last effort, but no, I'm done. He often jokes/complains how I would climb ninety-nine steps and 'give up' when one more step reveals a stunning reward.

Back at the site, via Austria, we settle down for our final night in Garmisch. We have no site booked for tomorrow but are now comfortable with the idea of just turning up (we are off-season after all). Two Italians are practically leaning on our caravan while they point at, discuss and laugh at our caravan Aquaroll water tank and Wastemaster water collector, it seems a very British feature and has been raising many European eyebrows, glad we are offering some entertainment.

Tomorrow Austria...

Camping Erlebnis Zugspitze, Germany – Site Review

Turned up on a beautiful sunny afternoon. I'm sure sunshine makes everything look amazing. Had we turned up in the rain I might not have been so thrilled.

Reception is a lovely building adorned with caravan items from quite expensive BBQs to blue and pink loo and oozing with leaflets for things to do in the area.

Greeted in perfect English we were guided through the booking in process. A tourist tax is an add on but includes a pass to use the bus into town and up to Eibsee. This ticket also includes a pass for the train from Garmisch also up to Eibsee. With the bus stop being right outside the site it was to be our obvious choice of transportation whilst on site. Directly opposite the site is an Aldi and an Edeka Supermarket, no car needed for the shopping either. The site is directly on the road from Garmisch to the Austrian border, at no point did this bother us, you are aware during the day but by night was very quiet.
Electric is metered and Wi-Fi is charged at €2 per day. Each site is fully serviced, complete with its own EHU, fresh water, grey waste and chemical disposal. We were unsure what the shute on the back of the pitch station was, site staff reassured us that it was a chemical disposal.

The site is like a gravel car park split into two by an open barrier. Designed to be fully functional during the summer and winter for the ski-ing season. They also have a ski and boot room in the facilities block. The first part is used as an aire with coin metered EHU. These pitches are separated by logs and sparse vegetation.

Through the open barrier and you enter the campsite. A little more greenery in this section but only slightly. Pitches are big and separated by sparse hedges. Pitches are gravel and have excellent drainage when raining but very difficult to hammer home awning pegs, we now own a number of bent pegs.

To take away from the sparse, quite barren landscape with Aldi and a couple of neon signed car dealers over the road, is the fact that you are surrounded by the most beautiful snow-capped mountains. Sitting at the foot of Zugspitze the views really couldn't be better.
There is also a small area for tents and 2 areas for seasonal pitches.

The shower block has free, very powerful showers with an endless supply of hot water. This is a relatively big site and there are only 3 showers and 2 privacy cubicles and 4 toilets for the ladies. Plug sockets are plentiful for hair dryers and people from the tents were taking advantage of charging one or two appliances whilst in there.
There is a small but basic playground for children and a small enclosed dog walking area.

Using the ACSI discount we paid €70.20 for 3 nights, broken down into €17 per night charge for the pitch, a tourist tax (free bus/train) charge per person, per day of €2.50 and an environmental tax per person, per day of €0.70. Metered electricity is then added accordingly. As it was warm we didn't use the heating. Pitched close to the facilities we showered and washed up there meaning we didn't put the water heater on either. We used electric for the fridge, lights and charging devices. Our usage was minimal.

Would we go again? Yes! Would we recommend it? Yes! Perfect for sightseeing in the local area with no need for a car, perfect for Motorhomes. Lots to see and do all year round. Perfectly located for the ski-ing season.

Austria in the Caravan

"Yeeeaaaaaahhhh, your brakes are on fire" was playing in my head, to a certain 'Kings of Leon' tune, as we descended the Mittenwald/Scharnitz pass towards Innsbruck. We have literally only travelled 43 miles from Garmisch to our new site Natterer See, near Innsbruck. Until the song started playing in my head it was a very pleasant scenic trip, and we were also being very pleasant to our fellow travellers, peeling into picnic lay-bys and judging our road re-entry to perfection to allow people to pass us. To be honest, we weren't holding anybody up, The Boss doesn't hang about whilst towing and we were making good speed up the hill, he was just in a good mood and doing his bit for pro-caravan, pro-British relations. Be aware though, friendly indicator, hazard light or waved responses are rarely mirrored in Europe, is this a British phenomenon or just anti-caravan, anti-British relations, a shame, we carry on being friendly regardless, we can't help it.

"Yeeeaaaaaahhhh, your brakes are on fire", oh yeah let me explain, the descent is signed at 16%, sounds no worse than some hills at home, but constant 16% over 4 kilometres (km, we are turning Mainland European) is having significant impact on our brakes. We smell burning, and The Boss, an experienced HGV driver, is telling me the brakes are fading more than he would like. You know the occasional steep hill in the UK when they have an escape lane that is just a sand pit, these escape lanes, about five of them, are like 100 metre vertical take-off ramps to the moon, plus a sand pit. The final section runs onto a flat plain of motorway so we let it run hoping the extra wind doesn't fan any potential brake flames into a caravan fireball.

We arrive at Natterer See campsite with a caravan and not a burned out shell, bonus. The sight is stunning and we decide to treat ourselves to a lakeside pitch, for another €4 per night, but this involves trusting our 'caravan mover' to manoeuvre our beloved van down a slope to the water's edge and the acquisition of numerous blocks of wood from reception for the front 'steadies', then we flung open all the caravan Windows, yes it was warm, but mostly to help remove the smell of burning brakes.

Temperatures of 28°C combined with the pitch setting and we already have a very good feeling for this place, we decide it deserves five nights. We turned up at noon so by 1pm the canopy is up and we kick back and relax in the sunshine. We have no idea whether Innsbruck is an industrial city or a tourist city, The Boss says they have had Winter Olympics here, and he thought it was where 'Eddie the Eagle' made his name, but no, that was Calgary, however, Eddie did once do a face-plant in competition here fracturing his skull and breaking two ribs. Always grateful for recommendations, a Facebook friend suggested the Hafelekarspitze was a good trip, thank you Dawn. Now, if you are expecting mechanical assistance up the best peaks in the Alps expect to part with about €50 per person, but on a clear day it is worth it. It turns out you can purchase an 'Innsbruck Card' for 24hr (€39), 48hr (€48) or 72hr (€55) that gives you access to every attraction in the City including Hafelekarspitze, so The Boss reads the leaflet inside out looking for the catch. In London this card would probably cost £500.

Next day, hardly a cloud in the sky, He is crunching his corn flakes with even more urgency than normal, "Come on" he says "We're going up that mountain." I drag myself out of bed while he goes to campsite reception with a fist full of Euros and parts with €96 for two 48hr cards that only become valid at the first attraction entered. 10.20am and we are on the free bus to Innsbruck for the 20-minute journey. From the bus depot the 'Innsbruck Card' allows us to jump on the next hop on / hop off sightsee bus for free that stops at each attraction but we walk the 10 minutes into the centre. Now I know why he had studied the leaflet the night before, "Look, the town watchtower, the card gets us in there" but we already sense a problem, namely that 15th Century architects never thought to fit lifts, I know not why, and seemed to prefer the installation of spiral staircases in tight spaces, ... I don't do spiral staircases, The Boss goes ahead and takes a picture, looks like I'm holding the rucksack while he goes up, then down, the 133 steps.

Three steps later, "Oh look, the Golden Roof museum," which is essentially a self-guide audio tour about Emperor Maximilian I and his reign during late 15th early 16th Century. Now, sorry if I come across uncultured, but I only tend to find museums interesting when you have forgot your coat and a monsoon hits, then the rain stops and I lose all interest again, so after clicking the occasional number into the audio guides to fake intellectual interest we exit. The Boss knows the suggestion of another museum will result in death by rucksack strap garrotting so tells me these two stops were just on the way to the mountain cable car. Luckily, he was right so I remove my hands from the rucksack.

The trip up the Hafelekarspitze involves a funicular railway from the city centre then two cable cars up to the summit, while cable cars give me the willies as they cross each support pylon these ones were not too bad, or maybe I'm getting used to them, not so the close bodily contact when they are busy though. As we enter each cable car we put another layer of clothing on in anticipation, some braved it out in T-shirts. The summit is stunning, we have to climb a few steps, so he says, it was a big hill climb to reach the top, we use the benches to take selfies on the way (eg, get my breath back).

The Boss takes pity on people struggling to take pictures of themselves and offers to take the picture for them, he now owns 8 iPhones on various networks.

On the way down a backpacker strides off onto the mountain, a few minutes later he reappears having thrown himself off, albeit with a parachute. As four more go past The Boss grabs his camera and goes in pursuit while I work on my Panda eyes suntan. From his lofty position he even got to see a naked sunbather but said the person was not 'his type'.

One of the funicular station stops served an Alpine Zoo, you've guessed it, that was free with our 'card'. So, we went for a 30-minute nosey. It turns out Alpine animals are quite shy, so after looking at lots of empty cages, a Moose, a Wolf and a big cat we head back for the train, which is just pulling out, never mind, one more in 15 minutes.

Back on ground level and we now only have 10 minutes to reach the bus station for the campsite bus or wait another hour, so he now has me speed walking, I hate being rushed, we arrive at the bus station to see the bus leaving the stop, trying to make our speed walk look quite normal to the bus passengers, who will no doubt be sat at their caravans when we finally get to the campsite one hour later, I blame the Moose.

The following day we need to make use of the '2nd' half of our 48hr Innsbruck card but without the rush of day one. There are two priorities, the Swarovski Kristallwelten and the Olympic Ski-Jump tower. We set off an hour later but The Boss still manages to find another two museums on route. First, the Tiroler Landesmuseum, how can I describe this, imagine you have entered a car boot sale in 1599, lots of useless old stuff, but obviously worth loads, forgive me for being disrespectful but 'not my thing', quickly followed by the Hofkirche, that housed the cenotaph tomb of Emperor Maximilian I, which was slightly more interesting. This guy wasn't settling for a quiet funeral.

Swarovski Kristallwelten turned out a good visit, but we'd hate it in the peak of summer. They seem to have created a museum purely to draw in customers, today that seemed to involve hundreds of wealthy 'purchasing' customers from India, I don't think Brits in shorts and flip flops with an Innsbruck Card is their target audience.

The museum was, in our opinion, slightly naff, but the gem (get it?) of this place is the lake and gardens where we relaxed for over an hour on hammocks beneath artificial clouds containing over 600,000 crystals sparkling in the sun. It was a bit like 'TellyTubby' world but oddly enchanting.

We arrive back from Swarovski Kristallwelten too late for the Ski-Jump tower, I blame the TellyTubbies. We spend our final day relaxing by the caravan. Our first taste of Austria has been good, plus we are informed many Austrian caravan sites are of equal standard. We also met some wonderful people here from Holland, Germany and, er ... Stockport. We leave with some excellent recommended areas to explore, which is why we now head to Italy ... not part of the plan.

Natterer See, Innsbruck, Austria – Site Review

After driving down the steepest mountain to get here, we are early. Another ACSI site and we're unsure whether they'll book us in early. It's only 1pm and a lot of sites like to make you wait till 3pm. Not here, told to go for a walk, find a pitch and let them know where we want to go. Natterer See in Austria is our destination for today.

The main building is very 'Grand Designs' and ultra-modern but fits in perfectly with it's surroundings.
I must point out at this point that this is possibly the best site we have ever had the pleasure of staying on, and I apologise in advance if I appear to gush too much.

As part of the ACSI scheme you are entitled to a standard pitch but can upgrade in increments of €1. We chose to treat ourselves on this occasion and went lakeside for an extra €4 a night.

The grass isn't trimmed to perfection and daisies are sprinkled liberally but the location of the site, facilities and views are amazing. With an onsite swimming lake complete with water slide, who could want more?

The site is quite large taking in nooks and crannies of statics, pods, safari tents, EuroCamp and tourers. If you didn't wander you would be blissfully unaware of anything but tourers. The other guests in other forms of accommodation are squirrelled away for privacy. The touring part of the site is divided by the main 'Grand Designs' building. One has beautiful panoramic views of the mountains and the other sits upon a lake which is back dropped by an onsite Alpine restaurant and beautiful mountains.

A walk around the grounds towards the restaurant, which is open to the public also, reveals parks and playgrounds, some hidden in the woods and some easy to find. The swimming lake is also open for admission to the public, as a guest you have free access. We found this one slight disadvantage as we saw a few people just wander across from the restaurant for a little walk around the site.

The facilities are by far the best we have ever come across. Separate facilities for the children, with smaller loos and sinks and an amazing baby bathing/changing room. Even the dog gets its own luxurious shower room.

The facilities for the rest of us are nothing but palatial. With private bathrooms available at a cost. The facilities for the rest of us are second to none. The block is split into a lower and upper level. With chemical disposal, dog shower, washing up facilities, gents and ladies' loos downstairs. Up a sloped ramp to the upper level you enter a communal area containing displays of miniature caravans and Motorhomes, the children's and family facilities and the gents and ladies shower areas. All doors and walls are bizarrely covered in what appears to be brown and green AstroTurf, which in some strange way actually works and adds to the modern, unique design. Music is played throughout the block, a big thing for me. I love music in public facilities. These facilities really do need to be seen to be fully appreciated.

Choose to go lakeside and you have a stunning uninterrupted view all day which changes with the time of day and weather.

Staying at the site you are allowed to use the bus into Innsbruck free of charge using your site pass. An Innsbruck card is also available to purchase in reception which covers you for entry into a lot of the museums and attractions of Innsbruck including a return trip up to one of the mountain peaks.

Looking out over the site towards the lake as night time falls and lights start to twinkle, encourage nothing but relaxation.

Price? Everything comes with a price. For 2 people for 5 nights including an upgrade to a lakeside pitch, local tax and green tax we paid €137.50 this did include unlimited use of the bus into town. Not cheap but 5 days of luxury of our birthdays.

Negatives of the site are few and far between. The shop is on the slightly expensive side. Wifi is expensive and sold in packages. We visited in May and the local cuckoo chose to sing all day long. The Dawn chorus consisted of a choir of thousands of birds all happy to be alive and living in in such a beautiful place, oh and the frogs, the paths come alive with frogs late at night. With negatives like these who could resist a trip to paradise?

Lake Garda, so hard to leave

We instantly like Italy, all the roads are downhill, ... yes? After climbing out of Innsbruck towards the Brenner Pass we part with €9 at the Toll Booth, seemingly for a tin of peppermints. We then begin two hours of driving downhill and now assume Italy must be two miles below sea level, the car is pulling the best towing mpg ever and the gradient is so gradual we never touch the brakes. The only slight negative is that we were warned about no overtaking for caravans on this Mountain Pass so we are once again reading the back of the same truck for a hundred miles. We think we are naively misinterpreting the road signs, normally a road restriction has the same sign 'crossed out' to signal no further restriction, we never see this so continue 'not' overtaking. The signs do subtly change and occasionally the caravan symbol is not included, we think this is a 'green for go' but being British opt for 'amber for caution' and stay put, plus, we haven't finished reading the back of this truck yet.

After three weeks in Belgium, Netherlands, Germany and Austria this is the first time we sense a difference from the previous area, difficult to explain why, the steep sided mountains are dotted with villages and churches and every inch of land is covered in grapes, so copious consumption of Italian wine is predicted ahead. The toll cost as we depart the A22 is €20.90, only a few more roads to the site, seems our satnav is even pre-Roman roads too, and we arrive at Camping Fossalta.

Lake Garda is not surprisingly a commercial victim of its own beauty, to accommodate everyone who flocks here miles and miles of campsites line the edges in terraced rows stepping back from water's edge up the hills, imagine tin box vineyards. They are however, very well set out and planted with many trees that make the site look more 'green' than some other European sites. Be warned, you are unlikely to pitch your caravan here without uncoupling it from the car first, you will need a mover, or a few willing neighbours, who really do help each other pitch, as you spin caravan 90 degrees then squeeze between trees lining the path to the pitch that is still large enough for caravan, awning and car.

As we walk down to appreciate the Lake a voice calls out behind us "Hello", oh no, are we on private ground, we turn to meet our fate, stood before us is Tineke, our neighbour from the last camp in Innsbruck, they left one day before us with plans to visit this area, out of hundreds of campsites we both randomly picked this one. They throw a lead on Timmy, the dog, and join us for a short walk by the lake. Later on, we jump on the tandem and ride to Lazise, The Boss asked a German couple if we could ride on the lakeside path, in German, he must have been good because they gave a hundred word reply of which he understood very little. Hoping they weren't talking about a family bereavement he nodded and smiled. We worked out that our tandem would be unsuitable by the lake so took the road to Lazise, having had the luxury of cycle lanes so far this holiday it was nice to feel wing mirrors brushing our elbows again, a taste of home. Lazise is beautiful on this beautiful evening and the beautiful people are parading on the promenade, joined tonight by two sweaty people on a tandem.

We return to Lazise the next day, this time on foot via the Lake Garda footpath, we pass many caravan sites close to the water's edge except for a fence and the lakeside path, although it sounds idyllic we would not like to place our caravan here, the fence is ... a fence (ugly) while a thousand people walk by and stare at you ... Ah, a zoo where you pay to be the exhibit. We tasted our first 'Aperol Spritz' drink, recommended by a German couple at our last site, who specifically directed us to this area, we could sit all day people watching but decide to walk back before we become too 'posh'.

Sunday, and we plan to do .... nothing, just a full day of relaxation by the caravan, watching our side of the site gradually fill up. Interestingly, to date, every site we have been on has been 60% German, 30% Dutch and 10% everyone else. The caravan vs Motorhome mix has been similar to UK which we didn't expect, not sure why, but we thought Europeans preferred the Motorhome. Generally, we have found people friendly, in four weeks, not one person has been rude, we have struck numerous 'site-time' friendships with Dutch people who put us to shame with their linguistic skills. We struggle communicating with German people due to the language barrier so settle for muttering "Morgan" and smiling each morning and "Hallo" during the day. Caravanning does bring down any barriers if you need help with 'pushing' or 'pulling' onto a pitch, people are quick to help. We attempt the local 'lingo' everywhere we go but that is normally - Hello, Please, Thank you, etc. We think 'trying' to speak local language improves the response. We are looking forward to France when we can manage much better.

After tea - 'evening meal' (we even translate for English people), we are invited by Chris & Tineke, our Dutch neighbours from Innsbruck, for 8pm Coffee by their caravan and then maybe some wine too, conversation flowed on many subjects and before we knew it, it was nearly midnight!! I hope their new neighbours didn't mind our chat. A lovely couple from the minute we met and always happy to talk as we passed by their pitch.

Monday dawns and The Boss is itching to be a tourist again, he wants to see more. I think he plans the car but he takes my hesitation about using the tandem as a "Yes" and instantly gets the bike ready. We take the high road again and jostle with cars and fellow cyclists, for some reason he has to overtake every cyclist we see ahead, men!!! First stop Peschiera, our first Italian Pizza and 'another' Spritze ... we even meet more neighbours from our campsite. Time to go back? No, he has another plan, "I'm sure Sirmione is only around the corner", he only ever half-plans, so we head 'round the corner' to Sirmione.

Sirmione is both picturesque and bonkers busy, we assumed it was going to be worth investigating as you had to cross a draw bridge to enter and it had its very own Police check point to enter by car, we thought we saw a 'bike restriction' too, but nothing about tandems, we whistled nervously as we sneaked the tandem past the checkpoint.

Inside was spectacular, and very narrow, in the 7 feet gap from shopfront to shopfront was hundreds of tourists and dozens of cars, mayhem, dread to think what this place is like on a weekend. Suddenly, a Policeman blew his whistle and gave us the 'curly finger', "Not Allowed" he snapped whilst eyeing up the tandem, he seemed to be looking for an engine, we wanted to joke our legs were the engine but decided to meekly look to the floor and head for the exit. We locked it in the car park and said our last goodbyes (just in case) before going back in for a better look around. We are amused by the weirdest things, so the best part of the day was hand feeding the birds whilst enjoying a very large beer.

We took the car free panoramic path back to the tandem, The Boss could see our campsite across Lake Garda but sensibly choose not to point it out because he later said it looked a long, long way away. The tandem was still where we left it, shame, so we had to ride back via Lidl, where we added four bottles of alcoholic ballast for the journey. This time we stayed firmly on the Lakeside path, which involved some deep gravel and big stones, but he enjoys the challenge and says falling off is character building. We stop one more time for tea (evening meal), The Boss says he needs pasta for the final hill climb from the beach to the campsite.

We leave in the morning, we have very mixed feelings about this stage of the trip, there is much about this site that we normally would not like, but we don't feel ready to move on. Hopefully we will return one day, but we guarantee it will be off-season.

Camping Fossalta, Lake Garda, Italy – Site Review

After driving through a biblical storm on the Brenner Pass we arrive at Camping Fossalta in Lazise. As we enter the site the clouds part revealing clear blue skies.

A man meets us at the car and sends us on a walk to find a pitch. Armed with a map off we go.

The site is on a gentle slope down towards Lake Garda. Reception sits in the middle of the site along with the shop, bar and pool. A lakeside view would be nice so we head down towards the water. There are free pitches but it seems everyone had the same idea. It's very tree shaded and seems quite cramped. Heading back up towards the top of the site it's far more open, not as shaded and not as many people. The site is split into tree lined terraces, we choose a pitch and put the legs down.

The site is made up of a few statics, seasonals and tourers. On site there is a small shop which caters for every eventuality. A bar, sits next to the shop and to the side of the pool.

Two facilities blocks are located on site, one in the lower end near the lake and one in the upper part of the site. Whilst these facilities are spotlessly clean they do have a couple of draw backs. Water temperature and pressure can be hit and miss depending on whether other showers are being used. The cubicles are very small with two hooks for hanging. There is nowhere to put anything down and very little space to get dry. The toilets are clean but toilet roll, hand soap and hand dryers or paper towels are not provided. The separation wall between the gents and the ladies was approximately 10-foot-high with a similar sized gap above. I wasn't keen on hearing the daily ablutions of men whilst going about my business. It did mean The Boss and I were able to chat one evening on our final visit before bed. Outdoor washing up and laundry sinks are also on this block and a washing machine and tumble drier.

The site is located next to a theme park area, Movie World, and various other attractions. Which, for our trip in May whilst the schools were term time, meant all was quiet. This may not be the case in the height of the season. Perfectly located though for families with children to entertain. The site is dog friendly but didn't seem to have a specific dog walking area, but with Lake Garda on your doorstep wasn't needed. There is also a playground area and table tennis tables on site.

Whilst this review may sound slightly negative, for the time of year we were there and the perfect weather with unlimited access to the most beautiful lake and breath-taking sunsets, we enjoyed our stay here and so far on this trip this has been the only site I have been a little reluctant to leave.

At a cost of €68 plus €4 visitor tax for 4 nights for 2 people, we thought was good value. Wifi is free with excellent coverage across the site and even down to the lake.

Two Tour Tuscany

The final eight-mile approach to our next caravan campsite site is why we chose it, we are winding and zig-zagging our way up a big hill with dozens of full-kit cyclists, they are panting with exhaustion we are holding our breaths in anticipation of each corner. The views are amazing both North and South, with that in mind we are ultimately a little disappointed with the campsite as the trees seem to block the view from any standpoint on the hill. The pitches remind us of The New Forest and the weather is 'scorchio' so how can we complain, I guess purely because we dragged the caravan up a mountain for a 'view' and we don't have one. Unless you stand by the pool.

The Boss is not too concerned about the site, he has earmarked this area as a 'sightseeing' opportunity and suggests we throw ourselves into tourist mode then move on. I hope he doesn't have any museums planned, the ones I've been dragged around so far are about as interesting as the nail and screws aisle in B&Q. The site arranges a couple of mini-bus shuttles, Thursday for Lucca and Pisa, Friday for Firenze (Florence), he calculates a value in his head based on diesel, car parking, tolls and especially the stress of driving Italian roads, then heads to reception to see what the real price is. It seems he calculated well, their profit margin equalled his stress margin and both trips came in €1 less than 'his' price of €40 total. Booked.

Today is Wednesday and we want to see a couple of places specifically recommended by the German couple back at Innsbruck. We jump in the car and career down the mountain like the locals in our best 'can't beat them, join them' style. Now we wanted to call this chapter 'Italy, endure it to enjoy it' but that conjures up too much negativity, to explain, the country is spectacularly beautiful in towns and countryside but you have to earn your enjoyment. Driving is a challenge for the unwary, if two or more cars are heading in the same direction, the cars in front are not 'ahead' they are 'in the way' and must be passed at all costs. Country roads, particularly Tuscany, have deep cracks and major subsidence almost continuously, what would require a total closure in the UK just gets a 50kph (31mph) speed restriction here, and that's another oddity, speed limits in some residential areas can be 60kph then in the middle of nowhere with only an olive tree to crash into it can be 50kph.

After stopping for dinner (butties in the car) we arrive in Volterra and our first chance to soak up the architecture of Tuscany. A walled mountaintop town with centuries of history to explore and view. Once again, we are entertained by a sideshow, namely a Frenchman going ballistic, in English (we like to hear 'ballistic' in a 2nd language) in the tourist office having just purchased a ticket to view the church, was now denied entry because of a private function. The private function was an American wedding and the bride had just turned up, clearly the sort of 'look how fancy we are wedding' that costs a sum we could happily retire on and will break up well before they retire, sorry, they've not quite tied the knot and we are predicting the end game. Shame on us, we wish them well. After spending a while longer on the panoramic city wall we move on.

San Gimignano is a treat. As you approach it looks like a medieval New York skyline with about twelve towers reaching into the sky on another walled hilltop town, apparently there were over two hundred towers at one point in history of greater height.

We grab some Pizza and sit on the main Piazza steps watching people take selfies while some old-boys in the corner play harmonica and vocally serenade and jest with the young kids, on the way out a shop boasts the 'Best Ice Cream in the World', we are sure we saw that on a shop in Blackpool once and wonder if the accolade has been passed on, we buy some to test the claim, it was good, but was it as good as Blackpool? ... Hmmm.

Rucksack is packed with water, sunglasses, water, sun cream and more water. Three other couples await the mini-bus by reception, it's late (Italy, remember!) we are provided with maps of Lucca and Pisa and the nice Lady even circled all the must-see places. Lots of circles on the Lucca map, but ominously, only one circle on the Pisa map. The mini-bus took a while to reach Lucca, the Boss reckoned he was using our 1950s satnav but also suspected avoiding road tolls had something to do with it. Unloaded on the pavement we took a picture of the mini-bus Reg plate in the hope we would see it again. For its size Lucca is impressive, we are finding that these places are spectacular throughout and not just in patches with modern buildings between as seen in UK. Entire streets are paved with the Italian equivalent of 'York Stone Flags' that create a distinct 'choppy' sound as cars and scooters whizz by at approx 80mph (Italy, remember). We treat ourselves to lunch (too posh to call it dinner) in the Piazza dell'Anfitreatro within a beautiful circle of buildings. After three hours admiring the town we are 'done' and realise why we don't like arranged trips, we can't move on, so we kill time walking the city walls and note boards advising The Rolling Stones are in town in a couple of months, another medieval attraction.

The mini-bus arrives, late! To take us to Pisa, the long way. We are dropped in a petrol station and told to be back at 17.30. One minute later we walk through an ornate gateway, armed soldiers remind us about current times, events back home and the vulnerability of large crowds. The leaning Tower of Pisa is instantly recognisable peeking around the top of the Cathedral, it is impressive, in the bright sunshine and against the deep blue sky we are struck by how 'white' it looks, like it was built yesterday. You genuinely can't take your eyes of it, but be careful if you don't as you will bump into people holding their palms in the air looking stupid to take 'that' photo of them holding up the Tower. We don't want to look stupid so don't bother, then spot an ideal opportunity around the quieter back area and decide 'can't beat them, join them'.

The one circle on our map seemed appropriate, as apart from another picturesque Piazza around the corner that was full of scaffolding nothing else really appealed to us. Probably slightly unfair on Pisa, but we have now been spoiled by lots of beauty before them. We kill time lay down on the immaculate lawns under the view of the Tower while we wait for the mini-bus that arrives about 17.45.

Friday, and time to go to Firenze (Florence for you British people). To be honest, three days of sightseeing is making us weary, how the people on those coach tours cope, jumping on and off coaches and traipsing around after a person holding a flag in the air, we will never know. It is hot, very hot, the mini-bus is almost on time and is bigger to cope with sixteen people, as expected we toured all the free roads in Tuscany to get there while the driver simultaneously made numerous essential phone calls that inconveniently forced him to drive 'no hands' to negotiate roundabouts and change gear. We are kicked out at the bus station in Firenze. The Boss, eager to demonstrate to the other passengers, now desperately reviewing their maps, that the British don't need maps started walking. One minute later we are walking along platform sixteen of Firenze railway station with sixteen others following us. We had to 'cool it out' and luckily there was no ticket collector at the platform exit and we walked heads high out the station.

We needed a 'wee' and The Boss doesn't like to use the McLoos if not a customer, but he hates paying €1 even less so we are now walking looking for cheaper options. To think, we once wrote a blog called 20p for a wee, you can buy cans of Cola for €1 here, so it's €1 in and €1 out. A decent looking restaurant beckons us for food (and a wee) so we stop and eat watching the world rush by. Today's trip is eight hours and despite many, many fabulous landmarks and sights we find ourselves a little bored at times today. Even if museums were 'our thing', and they are not, I doubt we would have joined the queues, of mostly American people, in the scorching heat. We needed some green space to lay down and chill but it was all on the fringes of town. We've definitely had our fill of towns and cities now, no matter how beautiful, think we need some downtime by the van. Once again, we kill time People watching.

The mini-bus arrives, eventually, the air-con is not working which for some reason hasn't instigated the opening of all the windows, it is now bloody hot, we paid in advance so I don't think our arrival 'alive' is a condition of travel. We get totally stuck in rush hour Firenze traffic, passengers are desperately fiddling with window latches that don't want to open, just at the point where a last text to the kids was being considered we managed to budge the Windows, everyone copied and air re-joined our lives. Funny, the driver must have been due to clock off, we went home the direct 'toll' route.

Back at the site and we have two new neighbours, complete with about five kids under two years old. Now we don't mind kids too much, we even had two of our own, but these five hatched a plan to synchronise crying so that no amount of time was spent without wailing, thankfully they had a night time amnesty that ended abruptly at 8am next morning, our planned downtime by the caravan, bugger. Luckily, they packed up mid-day and cleared off, we waved with big smiles. Love kids but I couldn't eat a full one.

Woke up this morning by 'The Boss' swatting Ants, "We've got a few" he says, followed by "What the...." the kitchen sink hosted a million, no joke, small Ants. He quickly decided if that's the way they came in they could leave by the same route and had taps on full, the next two hours was spent emptying the caravan and dealing with lines and lines of walking dots. No photos sorry, never crossed our minds to do an Ant Invasion selfie.

Our tourist fatigue has adjusted our plan to visit Cinque Terre, probably one of the 'must see' sights in the area, but we can save that for the next time, and there will be a next time. For now, we head for the French border, the Formula 1 Grand Prix in Monaco may force us to wait a day longer, so in the meantime, we chill.

Piazza People Watching

Day out on the bus from the caravan takes us to Firenze (Florence) 4 hrs of walking and lunch under our belts, our feet are in need of a rest. With the sun blazing down at over 30 degrees we seek the shade on some steps of a piazza. It seems we're not the only ones overheating and in need of a seat.

Call me nosey but I love people watching. I could watch all day. People eating lunch and grabbing time away from sightseeing or the office. Students sit and discuss the latest class whilst frantically tapping on laptop keyboards. Cyclists scurry back and forth like ants, zigzagging their way across the square. Some in a hurry, others stop for a selfie, why do they have to do that silly duck lipped pout? It baffles me. Scooters are dismounted and wheeled across with the engines still running.

Expensive Italian leather shoes, trainers and sandals all walk the cobbles. I can't imagine how hot those dapper city gents are in the suits and ties. Couples old and young amble past holding hands all armed with maps and cameras. An older lady sneaks a quick peck on the cheek of who I'm hoping is her husband, more sparkle in her life. Some people take photos on phones others with cameras, small lenses, large lenses. All desperate for a good photo. Brightly dressed street traders wander around, ladened with bracelets and necklaces, others waving selfie sticks, a bargain at €3 they tell us, unless, of course, you picked one up off fleabay at half the price.

Cranky children, the mid-afternoon sun has taken its toll. Dogs drag their feet reluctantly as they are led across the square. A street cleaner slowly circuits the piazza, cleaning constantly, cigarette ends, horse and dog doo.

The world passes before our eyes. All about their business. All with a story to tell. I wonder where they'll all be this time tomorrow...

Barco Reale, Tuscany, Italy – Site Review

Another ACSI site. Camping Barco Reale. We haven't booked. We've just turned up. Yes, they've got space, jump on the buggy I'll show you a few pitches. Zipping round it feels like a rabbit warren.

We spent ages pulling the caravan up a mountain to get to the site, once there, time to choose a pitch, within the site we continue to climb. Pitches hidden in trees, a truly shaded forest setting on the side of a mountain. We came for the view, it seems more like a New Forest camp site than one at the top of a mountain. We later likened the site to a walnut whip, our pitch was the walnut, right at the top.

A relatively big site but you wouldn't know it, with three toilet blocks serving the site. Outdoor washing up and laundry sinks, both with cool water rather than hot and no plug. A children's toilet/ shower rooms are also located in two of the toilet blocks. Toilets are clean and warm, it's 30 degrees outside so no heating needed, toilet paper, soap and hand towels are provided. Space is limited within showers for drying and dressing with a couple of hooks but nowhere to put anything down. Showers and coolish water are free. Sinks and hairdryers are provided but are outdoors.

There is a small mini market behind the main reception building that sells an array of bits and pieces for the caravan and plentiful food and drink. An onsite information office is manned daily with help and advice on what to do in the area and for booking excursions. We did a couple of these, Firenze, far too long a day for us and travelling on a bus with no air-conditioning wasn't much fun. The Lucca and Pisa trip is worth considering if you get chance.

There is a play area, table tennis table and a 1.5km fitness trek.

The site has swimming pools, a shallow one at the far end with spectacular views, with the recommendation that swimming caps are worn at all times. We won't be swimming here then. I haven't worn a swimming cap since I was at school and I've no intention of wearing one now.

The site is big and clings to the side of a Tuscan mountain. With plenty of touring pitches, the site also has EuroCamp style frame tents to rent, which are on quite small pitches and shaded by tree cover. There are also safari tents and static style lodges for hire. An onsite restaurant serves meals in the evenings and a small snack bar, poolside, where you can grab a lolly or a drink.

Wifi is free, although temperamental, and needs to be signed into very regularly.

Would we pull a big white box up the side of a mountain that cyclists train on and come again? Whilst it is a lovely site, we didn't get the mountain side views we were hoping for and didn't really see a pitch that did. What we did get was a beautifully peaceful forest setting with birds and lizards in abundance. We did also wake one morning to find squatters had moved in, ants! In their thousands. They then returned en masse later that evening for invasion number 2. Go armed with ant spray.

For 5 nights for 2 adults using the ACSI card we paid €102, with free intermittent internet.

Van to SanRemo & No-Go Monaco

A second significant ant invasion forced us to shout "We're soft babies, get me out of here!" and cut short our stay at Barco Reale one day early. The second invasion was realised after one climbed from my cleavage and waved at me, as if to say "You think this is bad, look over to your kitchen". Millions of the little blighters, every single inch of the caravan, except for the bed funnily, maybe after five weeks on tour even the ants won't go there.

Options were limited, we head for France but the geography and lack of sites on our ACSI campsite app force us directly to the coast road from Genova towards France and only two or three campsites we felt remotely suitable. The one we are aiming for is about twenty miles from Monaco, and guess what is happening in Monaco today? Yep, that's it, the Monaco Grand Prix, so we assume we will arrive, unbooked, to see a campsite totally full of caravans flying Ferrari flags.

First, we needed fuel, oops, it's Sunday and all the garages in Europe seem to flip into fully auto 'credit card only' mode. No problem, until we tried to follow the Italian language on screen and decided to leave with our tank empty rather than risk paying for everyone on the forecourt. Looks like a motorway fill up at €1.70 per litre!!!! The Boss calculated the consumption to the exact inch and shouted "Stop" to the pump attendant at the exact moment, and no, he wasn't getting a tip for cleaning the windscreen. The scenery on this drive was quite stunning at times and it was a shame to drive past Levanto, a potential stop, where we could have visited Cinque Terre, one for another year.

Having already paid €8 after 'cocking up' near Genova and exiting the motorway when we didn't want to, we exited the motorway a second time at Ventimiglia and gave our ticket to the booth, €33 he says as he browses his mobile phone, Blimey, we are using the road not adopting it, then, "No, No, No, More, More, More" as he finally lifts his head from the phone and sees the caravan that is following us, "€56", The Boss fainted at the wheel.

Amazingly, there was a couple of spaces at Camping Vallecrosia and a very pleasant welcome too, we set off for pitch 55, crikey these Italian sites are narrow, after waiting for a Motorhome who was proper struggling to exit we took our turn at two 90° left turns, first one, OK, second one, not OK, the rear of the caravan is just touching the bumper of a car, the Volvo is inches from a fence and the near side corner still looks too tight. The Boss jumps out, unhooks the caravan and we pull it around and recouple. We can't find the owner of the car, damage is no more than very fine scratches but we report it to reception in case owner complains. Great start.

After the wonderful towns and cities of the last site we have decided on 'downtime' for this stage, just as a bloke with a scouse accent walks by and offers us free train tickets from Monaco back to the town, apparently not stamped in the general chaos as crowds left the Grand Prix, so looks like another day trip looms. Today, however, we concentrate on a shopping trip for groceries and then lying in the sun for as long as we could bear the scorching heat. A cracking view, if only I could stay out in it as long as I used to be able to.

As we sat drinking wine in the evening we discussed our options for the following day, both agreeing that a trip to Monaco was not high on our wish list and another easy day actually sounded better. The Boss took that to mean 'get the tandem out' and decided we would ride to San Remo.

We are dripping in sweat, we haven't even got on the tandem, we have simply locked the caravan door and put the panniers on, it's about 35°C and not quite mid-day, we are clearly mad. To be truthful, the breeze from riding helped cool us down slightly as we rode down the promenade and cycle path of Vallecrosia, then Vallecrosia ran out of flat traffic free stuff, we shared the next five miles over a big winding hill with trucks, cars and scooters, all shaving the hairs off our shoulders as they passed us, then chased down a long descent at full speed by a coach that must have auditioned for 'The Italian Job'.

We came to the fabulous Pista Ciclabile della Riviera Ligure cycle path towards San Remo, (this is the bit where The Boss steps in with his cycling knowledge) and the 1.75km Capo Nero Tunnel that was bedecked with banners celebrating winners and odd facts about the famous Milan to San Remo one day cycle race, a better use of an old railway line you would be hard to find. The cycle path carried on past the harbour, full of millionaire yachts, and provided beautiful views stretching along the coast and the beaches and bars between.

Honeysuckle grows wild for miles (I'm back now - flowery girly stuff) and the heady scent seems to go unnoticed on male nostrils, until I give him a poke in the back and tell him to sniff up. Completely unappreciative we pedal on.

After about twelve miles we turned about, did a quick lap inland of San Remo then headed back in search of refreshment.

Aperol Spritz has been our Italian refreshment of choice, ample reward for a twenty-five-mile ride as we relax in a beach bar watching the Med in the deepest shades of blue. Monaco can wait for another trip, we are realising fifty days can't even scratch the surface for a European Tour.

Our final night spent chasing mossies around the caravan wasn't quite the sleep we'd planned before entering the final couple of weeks of our trip.

Camping Vallecrosia, Italy – Site Review

Another ACSI card site, again we just turn up. This site had worried us as to whether we'd get a pitch, the Monaco, only twenty miles away, Grand Prix weekend and we arrived to a queue of people trying to get in.

As luck would have it they had one remaining pitch big enough to take our 7m Pursuit. Just.

Not a very big site, but tight, a motor mover would be handy here. Pitches on this site are our first taste of tight, almost Aire, European style pitches. All our other pitches so far in Europe have been ample. This pitch has room for the caravan and the canopy, just. We parked the car on the grass to the side of our pitch. Only 2 pitches had this luxury. Others squeezed cars wherever they could. Not too sure the gardener was happy with our choice of parking spot. More suited to Motorhomes than caravans really as once in the site there are a couple of tight corners and not much room for manoeuvrability. Not sure we would recommend this site for larger vehicles.

The toilet block is to my liking. The only thing lacking is toilet paper, hand soap and a hand dryer. Toilets, showers and sinks are all separate, so you have to trek from one side of the block to the other in a morning to complete you daily routine, loo, showers then sinks. No privacy cubicles or hairdryers are on offer here. The shower cubicles are just one open space with no separate drying area or anywhere to put things down. I was concerned that my clothing and towels placed on the hooks provided would get wet but each cubicle is reasonably sized and things stay dry.

There are washing up facilities and laundry facilities complete with plugs for the sinks. Washing machines are available for a €4 charge and they have a member of staff who does it for you. Not sure how I'd feel having someone else handling my smalls that are no longer as small as they used to be.

Wifi is free but very intermittent, the best signal was near the reception area.

With the site literally on the edge of the Mediterranean there's no need for a swimming pool or play area.

Whilst the site is perfectly located for the beach, which is large pebbles, not sand, it is in a very built up area. Traffic noise and regular sirens from emergency service vehicles can be heard. There is also a sulphur like smell that appears at different points of the day and lingers for a while. There's some excellent cycling to be had in the area. We cycled along the coast to San Remo on one of our days.

All this taken into account for 2 people for 3 nights we paid €57.

Arrivederci Italy, Bonjour France, Howdy America

We have just discovered the most expensive road in Europe. We join the motorway towards France at Ventimiglia, Italy. We take a toll ticket, we drive approx 100 yards around a bend to another toll booth and hand in the ticket, €6, "You are having a bloody laugh" didn't reduce the cost so we just smiled, paid, and said "Arrive-bloody-derci". Never, ever, will we complain about road tax in the UK, you can pay the same amount in some European countries in about two days.

Italy has been wonderful, the places we have seen have been beautiful, but if you have yet to tow a caravan abroad there are some distinct differences in Italy. Driving; right of way at roundabouts and junctions tends to go to the person who can get there first, so beware, if you are waiting to turn across a busy road, no-one will slow, or flash, to allow you to turn across the traffic, so beware, if you want to make any progress in Italy you must drive Italian style and just 'go for it'. Parking; land seems to be at a premium in Italy, hence so many tunnels, when you go to the supermarket you are never sure if you are parking at the supermarket, the warehouse next door or somebodies private land, we always expected a clamp or ticket on our return with the groceries. Caravan Sites; let's just say 'cozy', if you have room for the caravan awning and a car that's a big bonus. If your caravan is 8ft wide only consider Italy if you are super competent/confident. We will return, because it's worth it, but for now, we move to France and relax.

We have a 'Zapper' in France, our name for the Liber-T tag that we subscribed to two years ago. This tag gets us through all the toll booths, without queueing, at 30kph and we only get the bill one month after. Probably even more expensive than Italy but at least we are robbed by stealth and get to enjoy that 'will it/won't it' moment as we approach the barrier and hope it will bleep and lift. Driving styles in France are similar to home, people anticipate the actions of others and generally allow you to filter or change lanes without problem, white vans drive like our white vans as do the boy racers, we feel quite at home driving in France.

Our destination is Pont du Gard and once again we adopt the turn up and see method as we approach Camping La Sousta. Yes, there is room, drive thru and find a pitch of your choice. Now this place is distinctly 'Forest', no one would ever describe this as straight rows of white boxes. Basically, you squeeze your caravan between any trees you can, in whatever direction you end up facing, no room for the awning here, but tree cover is dense so don't need it. You see lots of partners walking ahead of car/caravans making sure low tree branches are not about to rip off TV aerials or worse. A trip to the toilet and I am in deep trauma, communal loos and showers, albeit you do have your own door, I can't cope with that, I can barely cope with someone of the same sex in the next cubicle. The Boss, realising my anxiety, suggests we walk to Pont du Gard tonight and move on tomorrow, so we barely unpack or unload anything.

We set off for the famous Viaduct, near the entrance of the campsite we are approached and asked if we know the way by an American lady, we haven't a clue and between the three of us make a best guess. We walk on, two minutes later a car draws up, "You wanna ride down to the entrance?" So now we have been abducted by a stranger in a strange land as 'Sheila', the American lady, heads us hopefully to Pont du Gard. The car park is €8, Sheila has no desire to be robbed and we had no money to be robbed of, we get out near the entrance, win, Sheila has to go all the way back and walk back down, oops, we feel guilty-ish.

The powers that be, ie the accountants, must have realised that people do not pay to see the viaduct so very cleverly have built a large ticket office with many signs saying pay before proceeding further. However, this is only to 'go on' the viaduct, all the other areas are free of charge, and frankly, we want to look at it, not from it. The Boss has wanted to see this place for years, it is an impressive feat of engineering, plus equally, the entire setting and backdrop is simply beautiful. There are some 'outdoor evening event' type preparations going on today but this did not impact our visit, it did later as we sat in the caravan with very loud French narration booming through the forest, imagine a French version of Richard Burton, War of the Worlds.

We take a million photos and take time to sit and absorb the peaceful setting, Sheila has finally arrived and we use her, yet again, so selfish, to take a photo of us, our arms were too short for a selfie including the viaduct. The poor woman had the misfortune of being our first English conversation in a long time so we probably 'went on a bit' before finally letting her go on her way. Walking back to the caravan we abort the idea of cooking and slope into the onsite Bistro for 'takeaway' Pizza that doubled up as evening meal and supper.

The Boss spent some time showing off his spinning the towel and swatting flies technique before bedtime, funny, I'm sure the buzzing after he stopped was the same as before he started.

We move tomorrow, no idea where, says he will look in the morning.

La Sousta, Pont du Gard, France – Site Review

A beautiful woodland site on the banks of the river L'Alzon. Part of the ACSI discount scheme.

Arrival at reception, booked in quickly, choose a pitch and let them know which one. A restaurant/takeaway is located next to reception while a shop selling fresh bread, espadrilles and basic food essentials is to the rear of reception. We can personally recommend the takeaway pizza and fresh bread.

Sunlight dapples the pitches through the tree cover. Hard ground with a mixture in pitch sizes. Most pitches seem well spaced out and not on top of each other. A few pitches also have elevated views over the river.

To connect to the EHU we had to use our two-pin adapter. These are also for sale and rentable in reception.

The site has areas for pétanque, table tennis, tennis, volleyball and football with a couple of children's play areas dotted around the site. There is also a swimming pool, there is a dress code of no shorts for men, speedos only! Being on the banks of the river the site has its own pebbled beach, perfect for dog walking and letting them have a swim.

There are 4 facilities blocks on site with two containing washing machines. Covered outdoor areas for dishwashing and hand washing laundry. Toilets and showers here are communal with men and women sharing the same facilities. This is something I struggled to come to terms with, hence we only stayed 1 night. Toilet roll and hand soap are provided but the facilities are very basic.

This site is ideally located for visiting the Pont du Gard, which is only 5 minutes walking distance from the site and you are able to view it for free.

Wifi is chargeable with the first hour for free. Wifi charges were expensive so we elected to use our 3G router and our own 'Three' SIM card. We paid €18.30 site fees for one night for two people.

Would we come again? Possibly, but just because of my prudishness I would use my own shower and toilet. We also struggled with Flies at this site, but this has to be expected in a perfect Forest setting, plus we didn't have any repellent sprays or devices, so come prepared.

Massif Central, Troglodytes and Templar Knights

Legs down on another site. This time we chose a site run by a lovely Dutch couple, on the side of another mountain. This holiday is starting to repeat itself. Just in case I haven't mentioned before, The Boss has a love of mountains, bridges, waterfalls, old cemeteries, castles and war graves.

On route he starts getting excited. "Get the camera ready! The Millau Viaduct will soon be in view!" We are still 14 miles away and in this mountainous region we aren't seeing anything whilst we are down in the valley for a long time. Still I sit, holding the camera on my knees as instructed wishing I'd said it's too soon to get the camera out. Then when it finally loomed into view after what felt like a life time I could've said "I told you so!" My inner child stays quiet and I point the camera and click away. This way and that way hoping I've got the shot he wants. Chances of that are slim. In the old days cameras had view finders, this one had a screen in the back in 30° heat and in glaring sunshine the screen appears black, I could be snapping anything.

I'm on a promise, we are going to get a bit more up close and personal with this bridge in the next few days. Can't wait.

Going back to getting on site, each and every pitch is privy to a wonderful view. The site is stepped and up a very steep hill. He sure knows how to pick these sites; my little legs don't do hills. Once again communal facilities, I choose to use our bathroom in the caravan. Strange man noises in the next cubicle make me shudder.

A trip out in the car and we drive to what from the caravan appears to be a huge spit of rock looming up out of the ground. We've been reliably informed that if you get up there there's actually a castle on top of it, Peyrelade. Negotiating a single-track road with very few passing places, we get the feeling it's either closed or we've got the place to ourselves. We parked the car under the solitary tree for shade, it's hot and another hill looms above us up to the castle. The fact that our car was the only car in the car park should've told us it was shut. It would've been €4.50 per adult to get in as it was shut and I'd climbed a good few rickety steps to get up here might as well have a mooch around outside, admire the vista and take a few pics looking back towards our campsite.

In need of supplies we head towards Millau, apparently the supermarket is near the bridge, hmmm. We pass underneath the bridge but there are no stopping places to take a picture. Before we know it, we are driving into a small village, Peyre, that appears to be half built into the rockface, he is instantly distracted and the further appeal of a 'gratuit' car park outside the village sealed the deal. Once again, we are walking up steep hills to view buildings that were built around the 17th Century. By using the rockface as the rear structure, classed as troglodyte, the residents had strictly 'forward' views only, which today, centuries later, was offering a picture frame view of the Millau Viaduct, an interesting mix of old and new in one spot.

Still in need of supplies we continued to the supermarket via every road under, near or around the bridge so hopefully The Boss finally got the picture he wanted.

No Lidl in town so we elect for Carrefour today where we have the usual 'Wine' debate, The Boss looks at the €4 bottles and I look at the €2 bottles, we normally buy a mix of both then he concedes later the cheap stuff is actually very nice. Today I win the debate and we leave with a 5 Litre plastic bottle of local white wine for €9!! The verdict? Very, very, drinkable, we have purchased local wine in plastic bottles on previous trips to France and are yet to be disappointed.

The Boss decides that being up a hill is no excuse and a Tandem Day is planned. As we descend the eight miles into town he points out all the 'oldies' effortlessly riding up the hill, "But Steve, those bikes all have electric motors" ... No reply. We ride into the centre of Millau, where, ironically, there is a bike festival taking place, and very popular it seems too. After pedalling through the festival with a few French versions of "She's not pedalling at the back" called from the stalls, we retire to a busy street side bar and order "Deux grandes bières s'il vous plaît" while we watched about twenty paragliders leaping off the mountaintop and circling with ease.

€16 later, the beer was good, but not €16 good, we set off up the hill, with a thirty-minute rest while we watched the paragliders now landing in the field on our route. The gradient on the eight miles climb back was within our comfort zone so we made good progress back to the site, where The Boss stubbornly insisted on showing the 'electric motor' brigade we could ride up the final, near vertical, hundred metres, while Hans, the site owner, shouted "She's not pedalling at the back". Grrr.

We came to this area with little knowledge and no expectations thinking it would be a transfer point on our general route. It turns out that the Aveyron area of France is stunning. We jump in the car for a pleasure drive, La Couvertoirade is the vague destination but today we are enjoying scenery. La Cresse to Peyreleau along The Tarn, over the mountain, zig-zagging higher as each corner revealed a bigger view, dropping down to La Roque Ste-Marguerite via a road that had multiple weight, length and vehicle restrictions, plus some French word 'Danger', "No car restrictions, should be fun" says The Boss as we descend single track, no passing places, gravel surface with sheer drops into the deep gorge.

We live to tell the tale and emerge onto the D991 running alongside the La Dourbie river and the 'greenest' water we have ever seen. Soon after we spy a village that appears to be perched very precariously on an overhanging rock, we go for a closer look. Cantobre turns out to be a very rare thing, beautiful to look at, beautiful to look from, no 'tat' shops or cafes, just a village being a village. Our only complaint? Two or three post boxes had English nameplates suggesting holiday homes, as with many places we would prefer them to be 'locals only' rather than standing empty.

By contrast, La Couvertoirade is a little disappointing. One of five local towns originally built up between the 12th and 15th Centuries by the Knights Templar. Although some parts are restored the village does feel as it would 'back in history', only today, each building is either a restaurant or a souvenir shop selling exactly the same as next doors souvenir shop. It was busy too, this probably had an impact on our disappointment.

As we exit the car park our car starts to make the most horrendous screeching noise, we have suddenly become the main attraction. After a quick look underneath, The Boss decides to drive on smiling at all our new admirers, then stops at the very first empty layby and stops acting so cool. He's convinced it's a stone in the brakes but can't see or shift it. We try the "See what develops" method for a further ten miles and two pointing villages before giving in and removing the wheel and the offending stone fell out from the brakes. Hate it when he's right, but so relieved too.

Le Papillon, La Cresse, France – Site Review

A site on the ACSI discount scheme in France. Halfway up a mountain with spectacular views from every pitch. We phoned on route to this site to check availability of pitches as our caravan was going to have to do a bit of climbing and venture through some narrow roads to get there. The nearby village, La Cresse, is quite narrow as you pass through, but is practically traffic free, we had no trouble with our 7-metre caravan and doubt that meeting another vehicle would cause too much drama.

Met by the owner and her humans, Annette and Hans, we were advised to go for a walk to find a pitch. The site is Dutch owned, as are a few other sites we have seen in France, visitors on site are predominantly Dutch too which means we are able to have some friendly conversations due to their excellent language skills.

The site is elevated with terraces all fronting onto a great front window view which changes with the weather and time of day as sunlight hits the rockface opposite.

The pitches are separated by low hedging with a mature tree between most.

There are two facilities blocks serving the site, one on the higher level and one on the lower level. The toilets and showers are communal and have washing up and laundry sinks indoors with access to a token operated washing machine for a charge of €4.

There is a terrace restaurant attached to the reception, which opens two nights a week. Serving pizza one night and an assortment of homemade meals from their main menu on the other. We ate there on both nights and the food was delicious.

Annette is very crafty and examples of her work are on show throughout reception and the restaurant with a few pieces up for sale. Fresh bread is also available by prior ordering daily.

A charge of €69.50 for 5 nights, this has been our cheapest site so far in the trip. Probably one of our favourites too. Wifi is free with stronger signals the nearer to reception you are pitched. Electricity was included in the ACSI price. So, no hidden meter charges to surprise you when you book out.

Would we recommend visiting Le Papillon? Yes of course. Being run by Hans and Annette, without doubt, the friendliest owners we have met in Europe, this site has a very personal, family feel to it. Nearby Millau was easily reached by bicycle and the surrounding area is quite stunning to drive. A very enjoyable stay.

Lazy Ladybird Days & Six Inches on a Map

Arriving at Camping La Coccinelle was the start of our last week and hopefully the start of a bit of Rest & Relaxation. We arrived and it was blowing a hooley. Shown to a pitch we decided against putting the canopy up and quickly retreated inside the caravan. We were feeling a bit of a nip in the air after melting in Italy last week, this was a bit of a culture shock and a reminder of the climate we would be returning to in a weeks' time.

Finishing off the last of the cheap, but very palatable, wine we gladly retreated under the quilt to sleep and whilst the caravan continued to rock in the wind during the night we stay snuggled under 13 togs of loveliness.

A lovely long leisurely lie in, we throw a salad together for a quick lunch, then, from the warmth of the caravan, watch the wind blow the clouds away. Jumpers on, five weeks since I last wore a jumper, back in Germany. Feels a bit alien wearing sleeves after the heat we've had recently. A short walk to explore the local village, Le Blot l'Eglise. A bit of a ghost town, very few people pottering about. In fact, no people at all. I had a mission though. A few things I needed to see. The church stands prominently and rather grandly in the centre of the village with a war memorial to the two great wars opposite. Round the back, the church looks a bit neglected and in need of repair with a few broken stained-glass windows and missing tiles.

L'Huilerie du Blot came highly recommended on the site reviews so in we go. Shelves lined with oils flavoured in every way possible, after a couple of tasters we decided on a hazelnut oil, bottle of local beer and a bar of soap, we like to buy local when we can, but local prices rarely agree with 'our budget'.

Next stop was the local shop. Also recommended on the site review. An Aladdin's cave of literally everything you could want. Not a word of English spoken, we manage to make ourselves understood by pointing at the rows and rows of vin rouge, vin Blanc isn't an option, just the odd bottle with a price tag not comparable in the slightest to Le vin rouge. By now the clouds have started to part, cardy's off and tied round my waist. I'm starting to wilt. In the space of half an hour summer returned.

Quite an odd evening, after six weeks of occasional conversations, today, about six people walk to our pitch 'just' to talk to us. It's as if the owners have said "The Brits look lonely, go talk to them". Belgium, Dutch, Scottish, French and German, hardly any spoke any English, especially the Scots (only joking) so the conversations were quite comical as either party got excited to understand any word the other said.

Legs up and on the road by 10am. Having realised we have entered the final week of our trip, we have also realised we should be slightly nearer to Hampshire, UK than we currently are. Oooops. The Boss decides we should do one mega drive and give ourselves the longest stay, six nights, at the final site. So maybe this wasn't the drive to test out the 'non-toll' method of driving across France. Let us be clear, France is a bloody big place, after a hundred miles of normal roads the satnav is still saying three hundred miles to go, ETA went from 17:00 to 18:00 to 19:00, "Trust me", he says, but I can tell from the look on his face he is doubting the growing gap between his expectations and the satnav's ongoing predictions.

We see toll road debates all the time, so will give you our opinion. If you have a Motorhome and plenty of time, never ever pay tolls, French roads are beautiful, fairly clear, and towns are easily traversed. If you have a Caravan and plenty of time our advice is the same but be aware that in towns it often gets very narrow compared to UK towns and there will also be trucks avoiding tolls in the opposite direction. If you are on a two-week holiday, just pay up and get on the motorways because France will be bigger than you expect and you need to maximise your holiday. If your caravan is one of the new 8ft wide jobbies, good luck and bon voyage, you will manage, but will have some 'moments'.

Eventually the reality was somewhere between satnav and expectation. The Boss got the distance one hundred miles less than the satnav, which had the last laugh by getting the eight-hour thirty-minute journey correct. We literally staggered into the campsite reception, too exhausted to remember any French, "Do you have a pitch please ....?"

La Coccinelle, Blot l'Église, France – Site Review

This site comes with really good reviews. Which we always flick through before attending any site. One review stated that one of the approach roads was a little hairy. So, as the Satnav took us nearer we were ready for it. The road had a few tight bends and a couple of switchbacks but nothing that unnerved us. Driving through the village, Blot l'Église, was a little narrow in places, but again manageable with our 7m caravan.

Run by a Dutch couple, Fred and Ria, the site isn't very big and welcomes tents, tourers and motorhomes. We are walked onto site by Ria, and shown the facilities then onto choose a pitch. Pitches are spacious, grass and separated for privacy by beech hedging. There are a few small static caravans dotted about the place for hire, all seemingly unoccupied during our stay.

A swimming pool and play area stands to the side of the site. The pool, alas, was empty during our stay. Plans for it to open mid-June. There is also a small playing field to the side of the play area. A tennis court and climbing wall for the kids are located behind reception. With a table tennis table to the side of the tennis court.

Facilities are communal, a dishwashing sink area and laundry facilities are available at a cost of €6. Wifi is free with strong signals across the site. The best Wi-Fi that we have had on the whole 7-week trip. A small restaurant opens six days of the week for a few hours in the evenings, serving pizza on a

Wednesday. We didn't get chance to try out their food sadly. A small library for borrowing or swapping magazines and books is located in a covered area near the toilet block. Dogs are welcome on site and must be kept on a lead. There is no dog walking area but you are able to take advantage of the local walking routes close by.

Within walking distance of the village where there is a local store, that sells everything, a bit of an Aladdin's cave, a bakers and a Huilerie, that sells local oils, soap, beer and other products.

We paid €25 for two nights for two people including visitors tax.

A member of the ACSI discount scheme.

Last days of the trip

A marathon journey, eight hours, no peage, and we've only done six inches on the map. One of the hottest days of the trip so far and I've been sat in the passenger seat with a French map book stuck to my knees having map reading lessons. I've no idea why I need to learn how to read a map, The Boss has an inbuilt Satnav, in his head. He now drives trucks for a living, he's never ceased to amaze me though on his ability to navigate to and from places without the assistance of a map or satnav. After following careful instructions, I still manage to doze off and have complete inability to find where we are on the map.

We arrive at the chosen site, very late, hoping they have a pitch. ACSI card held as ransom we are welcomed and told to find a pitch. More of our native language and familiar British number plates on this site. Being only three hours ish from the entrance to France from the UK it seems a popular first stop site on route to the rest of their adventures in Europe. For us, it's our final stop. We decided a few weeks ago our last few days were going to be a little bit slower than the rest of the trip. Let's see how we go shall we?

After such a hot day no sooner was the canopy up than the heavens opened. Everyone retreated indoors. We happily sat a while under the canopy grateful for the respite from the heat of the day.

A walk around Brionne the following morning led us eventually to a small Carrefour. Supplies for the final few days bought. After reading reviews and chatting to a guy onsite who sounded like Louis Theroux we decided to search out the local village. I should've paid more attention when he said, take a camera and wear good shoes. All downhill through woodland from the site, it's ok I can do downhill, I just find it hard coming back up.

The path leads onto a road, turn immediately right and the breath-taking view of an olde world French village hits you, complete with the heady smell of flowers. Bells start to chime; the Abbey sits peacefully nestled to one side of the village. Picturesque from every angle and free to walk the grounds, a Monk locks the doors to the main church as we walk past and gives us a funny shrug of the shoulders as if to say "I'm not doing overtime tonight, so walk on". Complete with bald head and white Monk robes he fit the scene perfectly.

For the first time since Bruges, nearly seven weeks ago, we planned to revisit some places we had been to many years ago, namely, Deauville, Trouville and Honfleur. Picnic on the beach was planned at Deauville, so after feeding as many 10 cents into the parking meter as we could, we spent half the allotted time searching for loos that required a few 10 cents more. Got to get rid of all this copper we are carting around. A massive sandy beach, busy but not crowded, with perfect weather made for a pleasant hour before a brief walk to the port and back to the car.

We dumped the car on the outskirts of Honfleur and jumped on the tandem for the ride in. Another beautiful port town with distinctive tall narrow buildings all fronted by waterside bars/restaurants. Big cobbles and lots of folk made riding difficult so we parked up by the water's edge and people watched, just in time to see an old boy fall hard on the cobbles, typical man, too proud to sit in a heap, was instantly trying to bounce back up, we helped his wife to calm him and keep him seated but were unable to communicate any further. Clearly shaken, and well into his eighties, Pierre was still perched on a somewhat comfier chair for a long time after we moved on. We trundled along the harbour footpath under the gaze of the massive Pont du Normandie before returning towards the car, via two fountains that The Boss had spotted and rode the tandem straight through the middle of without any warning to the unsuspecting passenger on the back. Me! Now sopping wet.

Another lazy day followed and thoughts started to turn to the homeward trip while working out supplies and currency required to see us back to the Channel Tunnel. We suddenly realised we had brought over £300 cash in Swiss Francs on the journey but never went to Switzerland as originally planned, but where was it? The whole caravan was turned upside down, twice, plus car, we both started to think it had been thrown in the bin when the Euros had been removed from the currency envelope. It turned up a whole day later mixed in with his underwear, he said that was obvious with hindsight, as all his valuable items are in his underwear.

The Boss doesn't do lazy days as well as me, I could see he was itching to do something so I suggested a short ride on the bike from the site. I should know better, five minutes later we have descended a long hill, that can only mean one thing for later, and found yet another disused and resurfaced railway line which we are now whizzing along as he chases down every bike ahead. We exit the track at a 2km sign to Harcourt where he says there is a Chateau. 2km up a steep hill and we are catching a group ahead so he is 'trying'. Only when we catch them do we realise one of the group is about four years old and amazingly climbing this steep hill, "Chapeau Monsieur" we shouted in our best 'out of breath' style. The Chateau cost money to get in so he lost interest in seeing it anymore and we turned back. The climb from the Abbey back to the campsite was, as expected, hard work, but in total we had covered about fifteen miles in little over an hour. After a quick shower we returned to our lazy day and one satisfied Boss.

Two days left, oh no, we don't want it to end. We thought about the Normandy beaches today but decided the distance was a bit too far, then Rouen, but having done both before took a pleasant thirty-mile drive to Les Andelys and its history scarred English built castle set in a fabulous natural chalk cliff horseshoe on the River Seine.

Once again, he has me walking up hills, but I took solace in the complaints of dozens of River Cruise retired American tourists not expecting to be the latest 'on foot' invasion army of this rocky, steep castle .... "We are not going up there are we"... We will let you do the accent.

One last shop, butties for the drive home, chocolate, crisps and wine to chase away our 'end of tour' blues and another splash of cheap juice in the Volvo.

Day 49. We venture nowhere, we start to pack some stuff to help an early departure tomorrow, then we sit. We talk. We reminisce about some of the minor, quirky or weird moments on this trip and they feel so long ago, we have experienced so much and it has been amazing.

Saint Nicolas Campsite, Brionne, France – Site Review

A 6.30pm arrival and we are welcomed warmly. It is also, probably the hottest day of the year so far and we've been stuck in a car for eight hours. Would we like fresh bread in the morning? Go and find yourself a pitch. No need to report back on which pitch you decide on.

Not too big a site. 67 touring pitches, welcoming caravans, motorhomes and tents with 42 static pitches. There are a few seasonal caravans on site too.

The pitches are grass, with ample room for an awning and a car. Nice to have grass underfoot again. The pitches are sectioned off with sparse beech hedging and non-grassed areas, which people use as paths and will walk close to your unit to get to where they want to go.

Mature trees and climbing roses are dotted about providing shade for the pitches next to them. Other than that, in summer there is little escape from the sun. Each EHU point has a tap for fresh drinking water.
For not a very big site there is plenty do here. A covered swimming pool, pétanque pitches, a tennis court, play area, bar, small restaurant and a library complete with comfy chair.

One facilities block services the site, with separate ladies and gent's toilets and showers. Each has a couple of privacy cubicles and a baby changing area. Toilet paper and hand drying facilities are not provided. Each block is cleaned very early in the morning whilst the site sleeps. A covered indoor dishwashing area and a laundry area with washing machine and drier for a charge of €3.80 each. The washing machine is industrial sized so worked out a really good price for the amount it held.

Reception offer bike hire and sell their own homemade cider and honey. Opposite reception is a small café/bar which has a small shop selling basic essentials behind it. Food is served and apparently the Moules are amazing. Not being a seafood fan unfortunately, we didn't try them.

Would we go again? Yes, we would. We used it as a base for a few days whilst the majority of guests during our stay used it as a stop off point staying for only one or two nights. A good site for getting out and about in Normandy but not really close enough to visit the war graves and beaches.

We paid €94.80 for 6 nights including tourist tax. All electricity was in included in the price.

50 for 50 - Our European Tour Summary

We've been home just over a month now and it's time to reflect on what was the trip of a lifetime. The caravan has been cleaned inside and out ready for its next trip, washing done and we're back at work, back to the daily grind.

Our 50 days for our 50th was the best birthday present we could've had.

We visited 6 countries, Belgium, The Netherlands, Germany, Austria, Italy and France. We enjoyed visiting each country for different reasons.

The architecture of Bruges in Belgium, the tree lined roads and of course the 'to die for' waffles that gave me the biggest sugar rush ever.

Cycling in The Netherlands is second to none, with the highlight of being able to ride into Amsterdam. Wanting to sit and watch the world go by and finding ourselves passively smoking from the Coffee Shop next door. Spending a lovely evening with our old neighbours, Sam and Marcel, great food, prosecco and lots of laughter.

Germany brought mountains and snow, fairy tale castles and medieval towns, a splash of history and a few quirky caravans too.

Austria gave us spectacular views, mountains and a splash of crystals at Swarovski.

Italy offered more mountains and tunnels. I think every trip out involved a tunnel or two. This is where the sun started heating up and we dipped our toes in the sea. Our first taste of Aperol Spritz and little bowls of olives in bars.

France, good old France never fails to amaze. Gorges the size we'd never seen. Pretty little villages, bridges, monasteries and cheap wine, expensive beer and no little bowls of olives.

In total we stayed on 13 sites, all very different to each other. At the side of lakes, nestled in the countryside, on top of mountains, in the depths of woodland and on the Mediterranean coast. Our total cost of site fees was €949 for 50 nights. We'd budgeted €20 per night so saved a little bit there. We towed for some total of 2636 miles with a total of 3726 driving miles altogether. We have no idea how many miles we cycled, I wish we'd tracked that too, next time... Will there be a next time? I blooming hope so! I'd do every mile and every site again. But, next time we will track our cycled miles. Next time, I want to go for longer, next time I want to do different regions, different countries. I don't want to feel rushed into moving onto the next stop because we have a deadline date to catch a train home. By the stars, we need to retire! How long have we got left to work...?

You want to caravan abroad, but ...

The UK has many outstanding areas and attractions which could easily occupy your touring aspirations for a lifetime, but for some, the need to broaden the experience or improve the chances of warmer weather, perhaps for the only holiday of the year, will see them eyeing up the option of taking the caravan across the water into mainland Europe. (*NOTE. For purpose of this article Mainland Europe will be referred to as Europe, even though, technically, touring in the UK is also European touring*).

The idea is hatched but something holds you back, the unknown. Breaking out of the comfort zone is the obstacle and how long it will take before you are snugly back in that zone enough to relax and enjoy the experience. We have towed our caravan into Europe on two occasions, the first time for two weeks in France 2015, followed by a longer seven-week tour across six West European countries in 2017. We consider ourselves novices outside the UK, and while many experienced tourers may say "What's the fuss, it's simple" we still recognise the 'first time' worries and concerns people will hold.

Remember how you felt when you first towed, nervous eh? How do you feel now? If you are still a nervous wreck then maybe wait a while longer before travelling afar. If you feel competent in the UK, you don't need to be 'driver of the year', you are already well equipped to manage a European trip. Apart from some quirks we will mention below, after only a few miles 'on the right-hand side' you will feel fine.

Below you will find our observations in the categories of 'Driving' and 'Caravan Sites'. Clearly not a full comprehensive list as you could go on indefinitely, but hopefully it gives an insight on the unknowns and demonstrates there is nothing too scary or massively different to UK Caravanning. Some things may appear negative but often that is because they are away from the 'norm', and in many cases, you learn to see the logic in the differences and wonder who is doing it best.

Driving

- **Ferry or Tunnel -** Many are vocal about their preference and your final destination and budget will be a key factor. We are fans of Eurotunnel for its sheer speed and simplicity, plus we get to stay with the caravan. Many others consider the Ferry part of the holiday and a time to rest. Both options offer easy boarding and a competent driver would have little difficulty on or off.

- **On the right -** Road design makes it difficult to get wrong, roundabout entries point the nose of your car to the right as do motorway on/off slip roads. Occasions to be careful are when you exit one-way streets or petrol stations as you are not already 'on the right' in these situations your UK autopilot may catch you out.

- **Traffic Signals -** Essentially the same Red, Amber, Green as home. You don't get Red/Amber before Green, it simply goes from Red to Green. The lights themselves tend to only be on your side of the junction, ie, on the stop line, one is high above your head and often impossible to see when stopped but a second mini set of lights will be strapped to a post on the right-hand kerb at eye level, so try to keep at least one in view or you will be oblivious to the lights.

- **Stop Lines -** This is a feature we struggled with for a good while, in the UK a traffic light will have a clear line that the first car must stop at and UK drivers are accustomed to this. Many European traffic lights feature no road markings at all and it will feel quite unusual the first few times you see a red light and wonder where you should stop, even though it is obviously at the red light.

- **Flashing Ambers -** Imagine the UK scenario, it's 2am and you are the only car for twenty miles being held by a red light. In some European countries you will encounter flashing Amber lights during the night or at normal traffic light junctions after peak periods. Essentially, these lights have reverted to normal road priority for stopping, give way or pedestrian crossings and simply require your heightened awareness as you proceed.

- **Speed Limits -** Know your limits for each country. Generally, limits are similar to UK for caravans, ie, approx. 60mph motorways, 50mph country, 30mph town but that is only a guide for your expectations and NOT accurate for any specific country. Speed limits will be set in kilometres per hour and generally signposted.

- **Speed Signs -** Another 'watch out' for unsuspecting UK motorists. Unless signposted lower, the speed limit in towns is 50kph (approx 31mph) but will not be signposted, the limit comes into force at the name sign as you enter the town or village. It remains in place until you see the same name sign 'crossed out' by a diagonal red line. At this point the speed limit reverts to the speed prior to entering the town/village without another speed limit sign, so you have to remember the previous speed limit.

- **Locals -** Just as in the UK, locals will inevitably drive at speeds they feel appropriate based on actual speed limits and any risk they are prepared to take over that. Notwithstanding any safety risks this presents, as a touring visitor you will not know where speed cameras are positioned or recognise them like UK cameras, they come in all shapes and sizes in Europe. Our advice, don't speed, even when there is a queue of impatient locals staring in your rear-view mirrors.

- **Road Tolls -** Fore-warned is fore-armed. Road funding in Europe is different across all countries and collection of funds is invariably via road tolls or pre-purchased vignette.

- **Fuel Stations -** Diesel is generally labelled Gazole and mostly you will serve yourself as per UK, occasionally there will be a pump attendant that fuels the car and takes payment. Often, however, you will encounter self-service credit card payment pumps especially on a Sunday and we found some of these hard to understand in a second language. We tried to fuel at cheaper supermarkets on weekdays as much as possible.

- **Parking -** A sore point for us as the recipients of a parking ticket. Do not assume no road lines or no lamp post signs means there are no parking restrictions, in built up areas an entire district may be subject to parking permits and notification signs may only be as you enter the area. London drivers may be familiar with this type of zone but many people will be less aware. We would also recommend you buy a windscreen parking disc, as many time limit parking disc areas require you to display your time of arrival in your windscreen. These are normally available in European petrol stations near the spares and accessories.

Caravan Sites

- **Booking** - Our two trips were different, two weeks peak period summer 2015 and we pre-booked exact dates and sites for the duration of the trip before travelling, booked via the Caravan and Motorhome Club we found this fairly stress free and probably a good option if your first trip to Europe is during school holidays. Our second trip, seven weeks touring, was entirely the opposite, off-peak, we simply arrived unannounced at any site we fancied, using the ACSI Camping Card site network and its brilliant phone App. Next time? We may not follow any individual scheme or site network and just blunder around. Off-peak freedom is a massive 'thumbs up' for Europe.

- **Stay Duration** - In peak season this may be dictated by availability and require pre-booking, however, off-peak (sorry young families) it is a totally different story to the UK where you say how long you are staying and pay before you pitch. In Europe you arrive, you don't pay, only when you are ready to leave do you pay. If you arrive on site and are not happy you can either move on to another site or stay one night and pay/move in the morning, which we did on two occasions. If you love the site, you just stay as long as you like and just keep reception informed as a general courtesy, then pay as you leave. There has to be something here that UK sites can learn from.

- **Pitches** - This differs by country; Italian pitches were the smallest and require a motor mover regardless of your driving skills. France, Germany, Netherlands, Austria had pitches only slightly smaller than a UK pitch but positioning is far less informal and you can mostly position your caravan anywhere within your pitch and face any direction. First time out your mind will be set in the UK Car/Caravan/Awning layout facing towards the front, stop, walk around the pitch, think about the sun, the level, privacy and position how it suits you, again, quite liberating compared to UK.

- **Electric** - Two things to note. Amps and Polarity. UK sites are normally 16 Amps and you happily run heaters, microwaves, toasters and kettles all at the same time. European sites will often be 6Amps or 10Amps and you will quickly find yourself tripping the fuse followed by the walk of shame to reception to get it reset. Luckily, you should not need your heater and we found cooking with gas, ie BBQ, released spare capacity. Invest in a simple 3 pin plug polarity checker and plug it in when you first connect Electric Hook Up, we have experienced reverse polarity only twice across sixteen sights which is easily corrected by using a hook up polarity reverse adaptor. Only on one occasion did we require a 2-pin plug for the Electric Hook Up, luckily, we had the adaptor but the sites normally sell or rent one if you don't.

- **Toilets and Washrooms** - These will vary greatly by site and by country, our view was that if we didn't like them we would use our caravan facilities. Across Europe you may find facilities that match the best 5-star hotels like we had in Austria, or you may find communal facilities where your shower or toilet cubicle will be next to one being used by someone of the opposite sex, toilet roll may be provided or not, sometimes half the toilets will be 'squat' type. It is a bit of a lottery and sometimes only a written review will give you any advanced warning.

- **Internet** - Similar to UK this depends on the willingness or infrastructure of the particular site. We found 40% had strong free Wi-Fi - 40% had cheap Wi-Fi or a hotspot near reception - 10% had extortionate prices per hour - 10% no Wi-Fi so we used a 3G Mifi router on these occasions with a £13 per month 'Three' sim card for 20GB.

- **Aquaroll & Waste Water -** Watch how many Europeans point and talk about you as you fill or empty your daily water requirements, it is an oddity that can leave you a little self conscious. Mostly, European caravans have onboard water tanks with a locking filler cap that they fill via watering cans, then they generally catch waste water in a bucket and water the nearest bushes to empty. They find our barrel of 40 Litres sitting in the hot sun a little weird and emptying 40Litres in the bushes is not very discreet, or acceptable, so you have to do another walk with everyone pointing or water bushes little and often. With hindsight, still not sure who's system we prefer.

- **Fellow Campers -** You are in Europe, so, you will meet Europeans!! If you caravan in France the nationality mix is greatest, predominantly British, French, German and Dutch. Further East towards Germany, Austria and Italy you will find almost exclusively German and Dutch. We actually barely notice any difference in friendliness of one nationality over another, it is similar to UK sites, 50% of people actively look you in the eye and smile and say good morning, 30% respond if you speak to them and 20% avoid all contact and keep themselves to themselves, Europe is just the same. We had a perception that the Dutch were the friendliest people we met but this could quite easily be put down to their excellent command of the English language making contact with them much easier. We still had some great conversations with Germans, Austrians and Italians when neither person had a clue what the other was saying. A personal favourite was a German recommending avoiding a road on the map by pointing and saying "Das ist shit".

Hopefully these observations will be useful to any 'newbie' European tourers and dispel any concerns on specific aspects. For most, France would be a first venture towing abroad and we would very much recommend that, unless you have better language skills for another European country. The experience is well worth any minor negatives you may encounter and remember, every night you get to tuck up in your own home from home.

ABOUT THE AUTHOR

Deb and Steve Ludford, a northern couple now living in Hampshire (UK). Seasoned campers whilst our two girls were growing up. In 2014 we decided we needed a little touring luxury so are now loving life travelling around, when work permits, with our tandem bike and our tin box on wheels. We both hit 50 (sshhh) recently and to celebrate our 50 years completed a 50 day European trip with our caravan in tow.

www.inpursuitofadream.com is a blog covering many elements of a touring caravan or motorhome lifestyle; including our trips, our observations, site reviews and product reviews, as we progress on a dream to travel more and work less.

Printed in Great Britain
by Amazon